Designing Your Gardens and Landscapes

Designing Your Gardens and Landscapes

12 Simple Steps for Successful Planning

Janet Macunovich

STOREY
BOOKS

The mission of Storey Publishing is to serve our customers by publishing practical information that encourages personal independence in harmony with the environment.

Edited by Cheryl Winters Tetreau and Gwen W. Steege
Cover design by Virginia Hand
Cover photograph by Jerry Harpur/Harpur Garden Library;
2000 Artville; Giles Prett
Text design and production by Erin Lincourt
Indexed by Pamela Van Huss

Storey books are available for special premium and promotional uses and for customized editions. For further information, please call Storey's Custom Publishing Department at 1-800-793-9396.

Printed in Canada by Transcontinental Printing
10 9 8 7 6 5 4 3

Library of Congress Cataloging-in-Publication Data

Macunovich, Janet, 1955–
    Designing your gardens and landscapes: 12 simple steps for successful
    planning / Janet Macunovich.
        p.cm.
    Includes bibliographical references (p.).
    ISBN 1-58017-58017-315-2 (alk. paper)
    1. Gardens–Design. I. Title.
SB473 .M2583 2001
712'.6–dc21   00-063485

Acknowledgments

I'd like to stand in tribute a moment to those who contributed to this design process and book.

To my family, sometimes the only ones who know when and how to redirect my attention, who have encouraged me, given me ideas, and straightened out my messes.

To Marjory Miller, Eric Nikkila, Curt Pickens, Megan Pritchett, Debi and Darl Slentz, and Barbara Thibodeau, who shared their time, thoughts, and suggestions so unselfishly.

To all my students who question me and force me to work with real world examples where viewpoints are difficult to locate and beds are in frustrating places.

To those special customers, for bearing with me through errors or indecision, because this book is built as much on mistakes as successes. You know who you are!

To the publisher who opened the door.

Dedication

To Cory, Sonja, and Steve, and the growing we do.

Contents

Landscape Design One Step at a Time

There are probably hundreds of good books on landscape and garden design. Chances are you and I have read and found value in some of the same ones. But why are you reading another one?

Maybe you're reading this book because you are an avid gardener who will read anything that relates to plants. If incurable attraction to all topics horticultural is your reason for reading this book, I hope you will enjoy the time you spend here.

Perhaps you have a garden that you rearrange every year, and you're looking for ideas to use in coming seasons. Since you have a continually evolving garden, you must already understand what I think is the enchantment of gardening: "A garden is never done." I try to explain the beauty of this enchantment to all of those whose gardens and landscapes I design and to my students. Some never really understand; they keep trying to make a garden that can be left alone for a lifetime. But you, already spellbound, recognize that gardens are filled with and tended by living things that must grow and change: Plants will grow old and need rejuvenation; the gardener's taste will change with exposure to new plants and planting arrangements. For you who enjoy the processes of growth and change in a garden, this book will be great fun.

Or maybe you are the person I had in mind when I decided to write this book. It is written primarily for those who have wished for a recipe, a process that explains what to do first, second, and last to design a garden. If this description fits you, enjoy! You have probably read a number of books and articles, maybe attended classes or workshops on gardening and landscape design. You've acquired all kinds of wonderful information and plants, all of which you have "on hold" in various notebooks or in a side garden. You're looking for the glue that makes it all come together, a comfortable method you can rely on whenever you approach a new gardening project.

In looking for this recipe, you're not alone. Gardeners of all descriptions,

For Beginning Gardeners

If you are brand new to gardening, the toughest concepts you have to master concern the plants themselves. To help you out, I've included some advice about plants in "Where to Go from Here" on page 144 and "Recommended Reading" on page 152. You should start there, or at least take a look at that advice before you go past Step 5.

from the homeowner to the aspiring professional gardener, have told me they'd like to have this kind of book. They were looking for "guidelines for arranging plants" or "help getting started." Some were anguished over having to move to a new home because they had been "fine-tuning this garden for years, how can I ever make another one like it?" Others said, "I have to learn how to design gardens and landscapes that my customers are sure to like." It no longer surprises me to hear people ask for this help, it only surprises me that until now there hasn't been a book that recognizes this need.

I made another important assumption about the person who would read this book. That is, you would already have some experience with gardening, even if it was only one season, one patch of ground turned up and planted. I made this assumption because most of those who asked me for the book had a year or more of dirt on their knees. They had gone about their gardening in an experiential manner: Try it first. This same assumption leads me to believe that most gardeners will try to assemble a newly purchased item before reading the instructions that come with it. It follows, then, that it usually takes one try at gardening to decide whether a plan is even needed! The pure joy of planting and growing is reward enough, and it can sustain the gardener for a year, a few years, maybe even a lifetime.

You can use the design steps in this book with trees and shrubs just as well as with annuals and perennials. Don't be afraid to branch out! Every step of this garden-design process is directly applicable to designing a whole landscape.

The 12-Step Plan

I've written this book so that you can follow my landscape design plan one step at a time. My 12 steps to successful landscape design are:

1. Set Goals
2. Establish a Budget
3. Think about Maintenance
4. Assess the Site
5. Make a Plant List
6. Choose a Focal Point
7. Make a Scale Drawing
8. Place the Focal Point Plant
9. Frame the Focal Point
10. Add to the Basic Plan
11. Outline the Garden
12. Adjust before Planting

Focus on your goal, a garden or total landscape design. When I ask my students, customers, and friends what they think of when they hear the word "design," they generally focus on the paper on which the garden is laid out or the task of choosing plants and drawing out the plan. Although deciding where each plant will go and drawing the plan are important parts of the design, they are not the entire design process. You can skip straight to the drawing steps in this book, but I'd advise you first to become acquainted with the earlier chapters.

What should you do first when you decide to design a garden? The amount of information to be considered can be overwhelming: costs, time required to make the garden, which nurseries should supply the plants. All these things are worth considering, but it's useless to try to think about everything at once.

Take one step at a time. Through the first four steps in this design process, you will be thinking and listening, not drawing. You won't need graph paper until you're halfway through the process, although you will probably have to take notes while you and any others involved in the garden are developing ideas. A finished design drawing may be beautiful graphic art, but if the bases that you'll cover in the first four steps aren't incorporated in the design, it's not necessarily going to be a good garden.

Steps 1 through 4 are the heart of a design. You learn to ask some simple questions. You gather some essential information about the place where the garden will be. You may be surprised at some of the answers and insights you get. I know that always I am!

In Steps 5 through 12, you'll be able to take all those facts and insights and put them together into a winning garden. Selecting plants, visualizing the garden, drawing . . . everything comes together one step at a time.

Whether it's your own yard that you garden, or you are in a position where others ask you to garden for them, this garden-design process will give you a hand. Every step of the way, it applies equally to the home gardener, to the professional garden designer, and to all those in between. Throughout the book you will find references to customers and the person who will use the garden and landscape. Those references are not there to alienate you if you are designing your own garden, they're there to remind others of a point of view that could be missed, or a way to apply an idea to a garden that's not your own. It can even help you with your own garden, so that you treat yourself as your own best customer.

This Book Has Enduring Qualities

If you do intend to design gardens only for yourself, I would warn you to beware. Every beautiful garden you plant will increase the amount of respect and attention you get from your friends and neighbors. As one customer of mine put it, "Three years ago, the only plant I knew for certain was a lilac bush, and I only knew that when the flowers were there. Now I grow dozens of different plants, trees, and shrubs, and everyone in the neighborhood asks me questions, even in the dead of winter. I'm quite the celebrity, and you know what? I like it! I've even added books to my library just to help me look up answers for the neighbors."

So you may come back to this book in a year or two for help in designing your neighbor's garden, a relative's landscape, even flower beds for friends at work whose homes you've never seen. In that case, you will need some help to remember the person who will use this garden, because it's entirely too easy to fall into the trap of projecting your own likes and dislikes on someone else. I know. Some of the worst gardening mistakes I've made have been in gardens for my closest friends and relatives! Fortunate, you might think. Avoidable, I say.

This book spells out a way to design a garden, draw up a plan, and then evaluate the garden's success. With it, you can enjoy the fun of designing a successful garden, understanding why it worked, and you can duplicate the success and create beautiful landscapes.

That's where the satisfaction comes, and that's where we're heading in this book.

Cooking Up a Design

This book is a recipe. Recipes tend to be concise sets of commands without explanations. Take the recipe step "Stir thoroughly," for instance. It is expected that you will simply stir well, no questions asked. If you want to understand why stirring well is important to certain mixtures, you consult other cooking books or take a class.

Those who must follow the recipe appreciate this brevity. I assume that some gardeners who read this book will want that same format, but others will want to know "Why? What happens if I don't do this or do it differently?" I have adopted a format that will work for both recipe user and "tell-me-why"

designer. Each chapter of this book is a step in the recipe. The first few paragraphs of each chapter give the recipe step. Those who simply want to know "What next?" can read the beginning of each chapter. Readers who want to understand "Why?" can read the entire chapter.

As in any recipe, this is not the only route to follow. There are many recipes for meatloaf; there are at least as many ways to design. If you have not yet found a favorite, this one is written for you. Once you've mastered this method you can improvise special situations. You may find that your talent grows along with your gardens and you develop a unique approach. In the end, you'll be able to use the table of contents as a quick reference, like a recipe card.

You deserve a wonderful landscape. Have fun designing it!

1 Set Goals

The first step to successful landscape design is to set goals. Start by asking yourself, "Why do I want a garden?" Once you answer this question, you will be able to make a garden that pleases you. In doing this, concentrate on the important people—yourself!, or whoever commissioned or will use the garden. Along the way, don't forget the secondary users.

Usually when I ask someone, "Why do you want this garden?" the first response is a quizzical stare. I imagine their thoughts run something like this: "Why in heaven's name would someone ask why? I already know what I want! And even if I were designing for someone else, doesn't everyone want a garden for the same reason, to have pretty flowers to look at?"

Asking "Why" Is Key

"Why" is important in any project. It's worth the few minutes it takes to clarify the reasons for doing a certain thing. The reasons we give become the goals. They guide us as we work, and we use them at the completion of a project to decide whether we have succeeded. If you want a garden to have colorful flowers from April through October, it is a successful garden if flowers bloom in it throughout those months. It is incomplete if it lacks bloom for any amount of time in one or more of those months. It can have a dozen other fine attributes, but if it does not provide April-through-October color and that was its reason for being, the garden is not an unqualified success.

This may sound simplistic, but it's true. Several times I have been dissatisfied with a garden or overall landscape after I planted it and watched it grow for a while. Even though I could and did make changes, it still didn't seem quite right. After the third or fourth time this happened, I recognized a recurring pattern of events. In each case I hadn't had any specific goals in mind for the garden when I planned it. I had simply planted it to plant another garden. I couldn't pat myself on the back for any specific accomplishment, nor could I make changes with any certainty that my ambivalence would be dispelled.

On the other hand, I have planted many gardens and have designed many landscapes that had clear reasons for

> *Why do you want a garden? List your reasons here:*
>
> - Provide beauty + Some cut flowers for me April - Oct

*What do you (or
other users) want
from the garden?
List answers here:*

- DRought
  Resistant Plants
- Native Plants
- Deer Risistant
  Plants
- Some PRivacy
- Some Fragrent
  Flowers
- Ease of
  MaintenaNce
- color
- birds +
  butterflies

being. When those gardens were done, I knew just where things stood. It was pleasing when I could step back and say, "There, that works fine." It was no problem even if I had to say, "It's not quite right." I could go back to the original goals for some direction in making changes.

LIST YOUR REASONS

In order to feel successful or to have direction for changes, do this up-front work to figure out just what purposes the garden will serve. Make a list of reasons for planting the garden.

Notice that I say "reasons." Rarely have I worked on a garden that was meant to serve only one purpose. The first reason most people give for wanting a garden is to make the view from a window more attractive or to add color to the housefront. "Pretty" is a legitimate reason for wanting a garden. Once in a while, it's the sole reason someone wants a garden, but usually there are additional wishes. So in most cases it's appropriate to ask yourself, "What else is it for?" or to ask another person, "And what else would you like from the garden?"

DIG DEEP FOR ANSWERS

Getting to the underlying reasons for the garden can be a challenge. There are at least two causes of the difficulty. First, it may be tough finding words. This is because what we think a garden should be is the present total of all our life's experiences involving gardens. For each of us, that's a unique, complex, personal history. From the time we were very young, most of us have been exposed to the word "garden." For all of our lives we've been looking at pictures of gardens, attending parties in gardens, reading books that had scenes in gardens. We've spent a lifetime deciding what we like and dislike about gardens and building our own mental image of what a garden "should" be.

The problem is that people rarely take these kinds of impressions out of their minds and examine them aloud. You ask yourself or the person you're working for, "Why do you want a garden?" and it may be the very first time those lifelong impressions about gardens are put into words.

There's a second cause for pause when you are designing for someone else. The difficulty in answering to "Why do you want a garden?" has to do with normal person-to-person communications. The ideas we have about gardens may have been with us for so long that we take them to be facts of life. We've decided that they are stable, reasonable thoughts, cemented them in place and built up from there. If we feel deep down that all gardens are quaint places that smell nice, at some unconscious level we assume that everyone in the world thinks the same thing. That's why many

DESIGN BASICS

Spend Time on Step 1

I realize this seems rather deep and philosophical for a discussion of garden design, and I promise not to do too much more of it beyond Step 1. Extra time on Step 1 is justified, both in this book and in actually doing a design. That's because your success as a garden designer, even when it's your own garden, hinges on getting some concrete goals during this first step of the process. Great gardens are those that please the owner on a number of different counts. Glorious gardens are those that please you and make you pleased about yourself.

people have a little trouble responding to such a simple question. They may think it's rhetorical. They may not realize that the questioner honestly doesn't know what the answer will be.

Do you get the idea that you have to be something of a detective to complete this first step in design? Good! Does it already sound like a tedious chore? Bad! Once you've read this chapter, this step will probably take you only a few minutes each time you sit down to plan a garden. So hang in there.

THREE APPROACHES: ASK, GUESS, TRY

Pinning down your own preferences can take some work, but getting this same kind of information from another person is a real challenge. There are three approaches you can take. In descending order of preference, they are direct questioning, educated guessing, and trial and error. Whether you have one person to deal with (perhaps your spouse?) or a whole neighborhood committee, one or all three methods can be used.

Ask first. Direct questioning can get to a person's unstated ideas of what a garden "should" be. Try this approach. First ask "What do you want out of this garden?" This may get you one reason, a page full of notes, or a puzzled look. If you get only one reason or the puzzled look, remember that you are the expert in this situation. As a result of your own gardening and from reading this book, you know some of the possible benefits to be had from a garden. It's up to you to ask some open-ended questions that encourage the other person to talk. Avoid questions that beg a yes-or-no answer. Try some of these instead:

- "Where have you seen a garden you liked? What did you like about it?"

- "What are your favorite colors in flowers? Fragrances? What flowers, if any, do you especially like or dislike?"

- "Here are some magazine pictures of gardens. Tell me which of them you like and why you like it."

- "What kinds of things do you do in the yard where this garden might go? What would change if you had a garden there?"

Save your yes-or-no questions for clarifying, getting the most specific information you can. For instance, if friends or clients tell you they want a garden because they will "use" the flowers, you might ask if they intend to cut flowers for arrangements, for cooking, or for dried flower crafts. If they want "to cut flowers," ask whether a few or many cut flowers will be needed on any given day. There's a great difference between the sizes and layouts of gardens that supply a few stems each day for the dinner table and those that supply all the cut flowers for a hotel or restaurant.

Take an educated guess. There are times when you can't question each of the garden area users directly. A young child may not have enough experience to decide what he or she likes in a garden. One partner of a couple may be unavailable during the entire process of planning their patio garden. Or you may be designing a garden for a community building where so many people will be users of the garden that you cannot talk to each one. An educated guess is in order. Know what to watch for and look into. Look around for clues about the missing users' likes and dislikes: how they decorate, what their interests are, how they keep their home surroundings, what they do for a living. For instance, people who keep neat, orderly homes will probably like neat gardens. A community with a number of active environmental awareness programs may like to have a garden that attracts wildlife or demonstrates how to conserve water. Starting from an educated guess, you can look for gardens based on similar motives, and you can copy successful features.

Jot down features of gardens that you've seen and liked:

- Flowers for color
- Variety
- color April to October

*Pare down your
goals to the top four
on your list:*

1. - Ease of Maintenance
   - Drought Resistant
   - Native plants
   - Deer Resistant

2. Color + Fragrance

3. Privacy

4. Birds + Butterflies

Try it and see. An educated guess can be wrong. But it's better than trial and error. Sayings like "Let's run it up the flagpole and see who salutes" are humorous until you're actually in the position of raising and lowering the flags. It's expensive in terms of time and energy to try, try again. It can also be frustrating for the designer. The only times I've had to resort to trial and error have been when working with disinterested people in large organizations. The person requesting the garden was delegated the task and was just discharging a duty. The gardens that resulted were either very short lived or became long-term projects.

Imagine coming back to a try-it-and-see garden. Has it succeeded? The same people who couldn't tell you what it was for in the first place haven't had enough interest in it to watch others' reactions to it. You were proud to be asked to design and plant that bed in front of the library. You go to look at how it's doing. If it's not well tended, does that mean the people in the library feel it's not worth the time, or does it mean the caretaking committee needs a garden maintenance class? Without knowing what response it generated, you don't know whether it's winning awards, causing yawns, about to be returned to lawn, or turned into a lava rock bed. I love to keep in touch with all my gardens, but if no one can tell me what's okay or what to change in the try-it-and-see garden, it's so frustrating that I start avoiding it. If you have to use trial and error, do it only for yourself or someone with whom you communicate well.

An Abundance of Reasons

There can be too much of a good thing if you have a dozen or more reasons for the garden. If you are new to garden design, try to identify the top three or four on that list. Aim to meet those top goals with the garden design. It is possible to meet every one of a long list of goals, but until you've finished some satisfactory gardens, commit to only the top few. The more goals a garden must meet, the more complicated it is to

Timing May Be Everything

Sometimes the garden should be planned with absence in mind. It's not unusual to always take vacation during a certain month or to live in a second home from December through May. It's an important bit of information in the design. It may not matter if the garden lacks interest while the gardeners are away, but it would be inexcusable for it to be lackluster during the time they can be in it. Never take this point for granted, by the way. When the garden is designed to show off the house or yard and is in the public view, someone may well expect the show to go on in the owners' absence. Once a woman told me, "We don't get here until late April each year." Before I could even make a note of it, her husband interjected, "But that makes no difference as far as the gardens go! The neighbors love to look at our place! They keep an eye on it for us every time they come to look at the flowers."

design. You will need more knowledge and more time to find the right plant combinations. So for now, shoot for success. Keep your list short for the first few gardens.

Once people begin to examine their dreams for a garden, their visions are as varied as flowers in a catalog. Some want an old-fashioned garden to re-create a neighborhood yard they loved as a child. Having birds in the garden may be one person's reason to get up in the morning and come home in the evening. Yet another says that being able to cut herbs or flowers to use in the house makes any amount of garden work worthwhile.

To help you in your designing, I've included a list of reasons people have given me for wanting a garden, along with some explanatory notes (see pages 10–11). On the list you'll find things that seem sensible to you and some you might call kooky. Some items on the list may give you pause, and you'll explore those ideas further. One student has told me that a list is his way of identifying reasons for the garden. He hands his potential customer a list of abbreviated reasons and waits for the questions that come, indicating points of interest: "How can you attract birds to a garden?" "Can it be less work than mowing?" "What does it mean, 'have a garden for self esteem'?" To his approach, I say, "Whatever works!"

Look beyond the Main User

Don't overlook the fact that other people in the household may care more than you think about the garden. Look into this possibility with an open mind. You may be able to talk to these secondary users directly, or you may have to use other methods to discern what their feelings are. Begin by asking yourself or the person who decided to have a garden, "Who else will use the garden?"

Frequently I am told that "This garden is just for me. I'll be the only one using it." I can't dispute this statement, but if there are other people in the

---

Community Gardens

Gardens for community groups can teach you quickly about the importance of secondary users. Designing a successful garden for a group always takes more time than designing for an individual, because you must get participation or approval from important others. The committee that holds the purse strings has the ability to relegate the design to a file drawer; getting approval may be as simple as getting their ear to assure them you will take their interests into account. Someone on an unrelated committee may block approval because he is not sure whether the garden will interfere with his main area of concern; a few minutes spent listening to his questions is necessary so that you can paint him a clear picture. Volunteers may be needed to plant or maintain the garden; if you take the time to appeal to a wide variety of interests, you can increase the amount of manpower available to do the work.

List all of the people who may be using the garden:

_____

_____

_____

_____

_____

_____

_____

_____

_____

_____

_____

_____

_____

_____

_____

_____

_____

_____

_____

_____

_____

_____

_____

_____

_____

_____

_____

WHY WE WANT GARDENS

Reason	Comments
To create interest in a specific location	Entrances and window scenes of all types. Massed color at the front door creates a "welcome mat." In the backyard a collection of plants with year-round interest becomes a focus for meditation while you gaze out the kitchen window.
To enhance some aspect of the scenery	Some very attractive features on homes and in yards can be even more notable when framed by a garden: bay windows, statuary, gazebos, and so on. A caution: The central feature should not be upstaged by the garden around it.
To define a space	People need to create personal spaces. In a yard too big for intimate gatherings, a garden can outline or enclose a sitting area. Where a community restricts fencing, gardens along lot lines can give a feeling of ownership.
For cutting flowers and drying flowers	The garden can be a source of fresh flowers for the table or to give as gifts. Some flowers can be dried to preserve their color, form, or scent. With cut or dried flowers the gardener can enjoy his or her garden inside all year.
To increase property value	This is a frequent request though it is not a distinct garden or landscaping characteristic. The landscape would have to include a combination of features that are popular. Planning the landscaping and judging its success afterward might require an opinion poll to ask, "What about the landscaping makes a house more attractive to you? What kind of garden could sway you to buy a particular house?"
For fragrance	Scents evoke memories: A whiff of lilac is a link to a childhood home; spicy-sweet smells may be reminiscent of jasmine and the Far East. Fragrances drifting about in the twilight or darkness are especially pleasing for those who cannot see or be in their garden in the daylight.
For relaxation	Time spent in the garden can be a way to shake off stresses, to get lost in the smells, sounds, sights, and feel of unhurried natural processes. The exchange between a gardener and the garden can approach pure bliss.
To attract birds, butterflies, and other wildlife	The garden can be a private retreat, and the presence of living things in the garden is a signal that all is well in that little ecosystem. Living things are valued by many gardeners for their cheerfulness or bright colors: butterflies, songbirds, hummingbirds, small mammals. Food, shelter, or water for animals can be planned into the garden design.
To collect plants of a certain color	The inside of the house may already be full of a favorite color. What could be more logical than to extend the collection outdoors? What clearer need for a design than to put that collection into pleasing order?
To cover defects and eyesores	Hiding meters, utility boxes, doghouses, and many more unsightly features is a common goal. A caution to the designer: Most gardens attract attention to themselves. Keep this one low profile, unless it includes shrubs or fencing to actually screen off the eyesore.

WHY WE WANT GARDENS CONT'D

Reason	Comments
To reduce mowing	Mowing annoys people for different reasons. Some see it as a drain on time and money; others dislike it because it's boring. Some people dislike both the expense and the boredom. A garden can answer one, both, or neither of these complaints. It may be less expensive than mowing or more expensive. Its upkeep can require repetitious tasks or be more interesting. Avoid unpleasant surprises. Identify which negative aspect of mowing is the target and design accordingly.
To conserve or contribute to the environment	Some people have far-reaching goals. A garden can be a gentler use of earth than lawn. Contours can be planned to channel and use water that would otherwise run off into storm sewers. Plant and animal species whose naturally occurring environments are disappearing can sometimes be happy living in a garden.
Because grass won't grow	Even people who don't like to mow might be bothered by a space in the yard that looks barren. Low light levels or competition from tree roots may have caused lawn grass to die. It's challenging, but possible, to replace that barren patch with a garden.
To improve self-esteem	We all lead complex lives. At work and at home we can't always see the results of our actions and receive credit where due. The garden can be one place where the gardener controls projects from start to finish and gets some recognition for horticultural skill. The site for this garden is important, so that it can be admired and remarked upon by significant people.
For children to learn about nature	There is a lot to be learned from a garden. The garden can be planned to welcome children and encourage their exploration and learning.
For culinary use	A surprising number of garden "flowers" were originally brought into cultivation by people who needed the leaves, flowers, or roots of plants for flavoring and preserving foods. The designer can choose from long lists of edible plants to suit specific culinary needs.
For erosion control	A sloping area with water-worn ruts can be an eyesore or a mowing hazard. It's a challenge to establish and maintain a garden in this site. Give special thought to the caretaker when designing this garden.
For the satisfaction of seeing things grow	A friend's garden has been evolving for 37 years. It has always consisted of plants in all stages of life. The owners enjoy watching the change, the slow but steady interaction between plants and their environment. Some people would find this frustrating, would feel that the garden is not "done," but to others it is an essential quality.

household or others who will frequently use the area, keep an open mind a little longer. I have seen uninterested people become interested, with good and bad results. Their interest may be only in finances. They may have an interest or hobby that overlaps the garden area. They might be the caretakers of the yard. It's worth the effort to check into their feelings on the subject, because they may care deeply about some aspect of the garden, and they certainly can affect it.

KIDS COUNT

Children may not notice your garden at all until they have to wade into it to retrieve a soccer ball. But I've found that if kids are consulted about where the garden may be placed and what they might like to see in it, or are involved in the planting, they take just a little extra interest in its welfare. I've seen more than one young boy or girl become an enthusiastic gardener after simply being included in the plant selection process. What saves the day for me is a list of colorful common names for plants and a story to tell about each. Some of my favorites are adder's tongue, lady's slipper, and woundwort.

DON'T LEAVE OUT THE SPOUSE

The same case can be made for consulting the supposedly uninterested spouse. One example of spouse/garden dynamics involves edging. I have seen gardens with immaculate edges and gardens with sloppy, tall grass fringes. Not only is the tall grass edge unattractive, the grass in it tends to have extra vigor because of its greater leaf area, so it can send invading roots deeper into the garden than grass that's kept short. The kind of edge the garden ultimately has may be directly influenced by whether

the mower-wielding spouse was given some input early on in the design. To understand this point, you may have to get out a mower and take a turn around a yard with a garden. Until you've done it, you can't appreciate the enormous task it can be to maneuver a mower in and out of deep sinuses of lawn along the edges of beds. The division of labor when it comes to my own lawn is clear-cut: I strive to eliminate the lawns; my husband agrees to do the mowing until the lawns become history. Under extremely unusual circumstances, the job of mowing fell to me one day, and I was aghast at the amount of extra work our garden edges created. It was a simple problem to correct, but my husband, Steve, had never complained so it had never occurred to me to do it. Don't take the chance that your gardening efforts might be systematically undermined by mowers harboring a grudge. Ask for input from anyone who may have an interest sooner or later.

You've Completed Step 1!

Now, that wasn't so bad, was it? The first step is so important, it pays in the long run to take the time you need to do it right. When you've completed this first step in design, you'll have a list of reasons for wanting the garden. You'll be glad you have it when you draft the design. Save the list and come back to it after a year. Even if the garden is not ready in its first year to appear in the garden column in your local newspaper, it probably has fulfilled at least one of your goals. If it hasn't met all the goals, you will know which features to keep because they have already proven themselves successful, and which you can change when you try again.

step 2
Establish a Budget

The second step to successful landscape design is to create a budget. The costs of preparing the garden area, purchasing materials, and maintaining the garden vary widely. Decide what is a reasonable amount of money and time to spend. This will be the budget you try to meet with your new design.

Spending Not Just Money, but Time

Your aim in this step is to establish what the expectations are when it comes to garden expense. Though dollars are often the first expense category you'll deal with, don't overlook the time factor. It's common to suppose that people are happy when they save lots of money. But the garden may be planned to add flair to a party or provide a backdrop for graduation pictures. Dollar savings may mean nothing if, by the important date, the garden does not look and act as it was expected to. For this reason, some people have been displeased with a garden that I would call inexpensive. Others have been very happy after purchasing or planting a garden at what I consider

to be great expense. So try to pinpoint when the garden is expected to fulfill its goals before you look at a dollar figure to achieve that result.

Many gardeners (I'm one of them!) have a tough time thinking about finances and deadlines for their gardens. In my case, this is because I want every garden to be as wonderful as it can be. It's unthinkable to consider that something so paltry as money or time could hold up the garden: "Hang the cost and I don't care how long it takes!" This attitude is okay when you are working on your own gardens or with someone who is fully aware of how much money and how many years can go into a garden. One of my own rock gardens has been three years in the making and is still only 10 percent planted, and if I had to pay myself for all the hours spent so far, I'd be rich. Few gardens take so long or cost so much, but the possibility exists.

RETURN TO YOUR GOALS

Time and money can be easier to talk about if you use that list of goals you made in Step 1. If you know that the garden is planned to spruce up the patio, by what date must the full sensational effect

List your plants and the dates on which you need them to look their best:

be achieved? How disappointing to design a gorgeous garden and plant it inexpensively, only to realize that it won't be lush in time for the wedding that will take place in it!

Don't assume that anyone else knows your time budget. I'm perfectly happy with my rock garden, so isn't it possible that I would think you would be also? Having pinned down your time expectation, you will now be able to state your need clearly as you look in plant books, at the garden center, everywhere. For one garden you may ask, "How many plants do I need, what can I do, for the garden to look full by? . . ." For the next garden, you may ask, "Do I really need so many, if I can wait for it to fill in?"

Starting with Price

Think of your first look into dollar amounts simply as a starting point. Many of us decide how much money we have to spend on a purchase by shopping around. Once we establish what appears to be a reasonable price range, we decide which item in that range comes closest to our dream. Since fully assembled gardens are not available at stores or through catalogs, it can be difficult for someone who has never or only rarely purchased a garden to establish a reasonable price range. To help you out, use this comparison: The cost of a garden is comparable to and can vary as much as the cost of new living room furniture.

When the shopper finds the right furniture, it may be too expensive to buy outright. Layaway terms can be arranged, or the set may be purchased a piece at a time. As you design, you can find the combinations that add up to your dream garden. There are so many things you can do to affect the dollar cost that you will be able to do almost anything for almost any amount of money.

The furniture shopper may decide to devote some of his or her own labor in exchange for monetary savings, by buying unfinished furniture. The gardener also has an option that reduces labor costs: planting the garden without hired help. The horticultural equivalent of layaway is to plant the garden in stages. A garden purchased over time may even cost less than the same garden purchased all at once. And there is one approach the garden designer can use that isn't open to the furniture shopper. The garden designer can choose to cut costs by using smaller plants; the furniture shopper can't buy a small sofa and expect it to grow larger.

Finally, this analogy comes back to the fact that both time and money are important aspects of setting a budget. Both the furniture shopper and the garden designer share this important limitation as they negotiate for their dream: As the monetary limit decreases, control over time must increase. Neither the furniture set put on layaway nor the garden planted in stages can be enjoyed immediately. And furniture that must be finished requires a waiting period, just as smaller, less expensive plants take longer to grow and fill the garden.

TRACK COSTS

When it comes to proposing a dollar figure, you are in one of two situations: Either you have planted gardens before and can identify a price range based on your experience, or you have not planted before. If you've planted gardens before, you need to keep track of costs when you plant. Keep a log of materials purchased and hours spent. Even if you do not pay wages to anyone, assign a dollar figure for an hour's work. Add all the dollars and dollar-hours and divide by the size of the garden to develop a price per square foot or square yard for each garden planted. You will end up with a range of prices for planting a garden.

Propose a figure based on where within the range you think this garden will fall.

Propose this figure to whom? To yourself. To anyone you share expenses with. To the person who will pay for the garden. All of these people deserve some idea of what they're getting themselves into. Sometimes the dollar figure leaves people short of breath, sometimes they smile. How else will you know whether to design parsimoniously or with abandon?

Turn reasons into numbers. For those who have never planted a garden before and must now establish a price proposal, use your list of reasons for the garden. Turn the reasons into numbers,

A Starting Point, Not an Estimate

When I explain my costing-out formula to students in the gardening business, they sometimes gasp, "Impossible! You won't let us jump ahead in the process to figure out how large the garden will be or exactly what plants go in it, and yet you want us to give someone an estimate?!" This step in the design process is not an estimate. This is proposing a starting point, establishing a reasonable budget to help you make decisions as you design. An estimate comes after the design is done. If the designer has done a good job, the finished design will yield a garden that can fulfill the goals within or close to the budget.

if you can. For example, if the garden is to provide privacy, look into the cost of a privacy fence. Ask, "Since this garden will provide privacy, is it worth what a privacy fence would cost?" Then you have a starting point. If the garden is meant to provide a pretty view from a window, check the cost of draperies or blinds. A garden meant to decorate an outside entertaining area might be compared to the cost of buying floral arrangements for that area for a season. This strategy can even amount to a selling point when you have to convince someone that the cost is reasonable. If the garden can achieve its goals for the same amount or less than a nongarden solution would cost, isn't that an additional benefit? Might it even buy you some physical help, when it's time to plant, if your budget-conscious spouse views the garden as a "deal"?

BALANCE THE BUDGET

Now put the time and dollar expectations side by side: "I'm looking for a garden that will dress up the patio, feed the birds, and give me dried flowers by this time next year; I want to spend less than $300.00 in all." This is your budget. If you have designed and planted some gardens in the past, you can draw some conclusions about whether the two components are compatible. Or you may not have enough experience with gardens to make any judgments. In either case, you can ask yourself or that important other person some questions to help you balance time and money while you design. Establish whether either or both components of the budget are flexible. Here's one approach: "What if the entire garden cannot be planted in a single year for this figure?" This opens the door to looking into the variables in creating a garden. Following are some of the topics you may get into if you are not the only one holding the purse strings.

Put time and money together to create a budget. List price ranges here for various stages of the garden:

"If the dollars we discussed are not firm, why did we talk about that at all?" The main goal of the design process is to create a garden that fits the list of reasons you gave for wanting the garden. For any list of reasons, a number of garden designs might be developed, some more expensive than others. I establish a budget that I can use throughout the design process, to keep costs in line.

"It might cost more?" It can happen. For instance, though budget constraints would prompt you to be on the lookout for less expensive sizes and varieties of plants, there may not be options in every case. Sometimes the only way to make some part of the garden do what it's intended to do is to set the budget aside, finish that portion of the design, and see whether the extra expense is worth it.

"You mean it doesn't have to be done all at once?" Even a fine botanical garden can be developed and planted in stages and can look good throughout the process. It simply has to be designed for gradual development.

Don't Jump the Gun

You may also ask or be asked, "What can we do to cut down on the cost?" In anything that involves time and money, there are ways to cut costs. But you haven't got any costs yet, you're just setting a budget. While you're designing, you'll be on the lookout for any ways to meet or beat the budget. It's better to finish both design and estimate before getting specific about any cost-reducing option and how much money and time would actually be saved. For instance, using smaller plants can save on material expenses, but without knowing the particular plants you'll be using, it's impossible to know whether smaller sizes are available and what the total savings could be.

Throughout the rest of this book I'll remind you to think about costs and to discuss various options in terms of their impact on cost.

MAKE A 3-YEAR PLAN

You may have big ideas for your landscape, but not a big budget. That's okay. Many landscapes are developed and planted in stages. Think about what you can afford now, and list those plants and related costs under "Year 1" below. Do the same for years 2 and 3, and track this year's costs to see how close you've come to your budget.

Year I

_____

_____

_____

_____

_____

_____

_____

Year 2

_____

_____

_____

_____

_____

_____

_____

Year 3

_____

_____

_____

_____

_____

_____

_____

3 Think about Maintenance

The third step to successful landscape design is to identify who will take care of the garden. Think about their experience level and pin down the number of hours per week that can be spent on maintenance.

Maintenance can make or break a garden. So, whether you are designing your own or another person's garden, the caretaker is an important individual to consider. It's easy to look ahead at maintenance and keep the requirements within reason. If you don't give it some thought, the most trivial things can add up to make the garden too much of a chore. Then, even you will probably neglect it. A neglected garden reverts with incredible speed to a naturalized state, a sight you can preview by looking at any undeveloped lot in your area. It's not a pretty sight, is it?

Planning for Garden Care

People involved in caring for the garden may not recognize the fact that you took the time to plan for their welfare. "Conscript laborers," as one friend refers to her teenage children, are not going to be very happy about any amount of work that has to be done when they long to be elsewhere. Your forethought in this case simply reduces the number of hours you have to spend as boss over a chain gang.

Then there are the caretakers who are new to gardening. These people will simply feel that the garden is "okay." That's actually a plus, since you avoid the negative impact of disgruntled mowers or lost referrals. Still, it feels so much better to be appreciated for your efforts! Here's a dark confession: Sometimes, when working with a new gardener, I consider deliberately withholding my best caretaker-consideration tactics and letting the person learn that gardening can be hard work. Then, I imagine, I would do a better garden next year and they would really appreciate me. Just passing thoughts, though. I love gardens and what they do for people too much. I could never take the chance that a potential gardener might be turned off.

You'll get full value for your work in this step when the caretaker of the garden is you, or someone with previous gardening experience. Experienced gardeners, who already know that some

---

Take a look at your goals list. Which are high maintenance and which are low?

HIGH MAINTENANCE:

1. _____

2. _____

3. _____

4. _____

LOW MAINTENANCE:

1. _____

2. _____

3. _____

4. _____

List each plant and arrangement in your design. Then check off those that you or the caretaker can handle.

Don't Take Shortcuts

A student in a mixed class of home gardeners and professional garden designers once posed this question: "What difference does it make to me whether the caretaker can or can't take care of the garden easily? If I were hired to design and plant a garden, once that's done, that's done." As it turned out, I didn't have to answer the question; the class answered for me. The questioner was told, "That's exactly what is wrong with businesses today! No one wants to take responsibility for long-term performance. Do you think if the garden you designed and planted is overgrown or dying after a few months, that you'll get any referrals from me? Do you think that anyone will even bother to ask who did that garden? How long before your reputation catches up with you, and there are no other gardens for you?" The moral of this story: Don't take short-cuts. Plan your garden carefully whether it is for your pleasure or someone else's, and keep maintenance at the front of your mind as you plan.

gardens are more trouble than they're worth, will recognize the things you've done to make the job easier. They might thank you. They may even tell others about the pleasures of working in a garden you designed.

EXPERIENCE COUNTS

Begin this step of the design process with the question, "Who will be taking care of the garden?" If it's not you, the experience level of the caretaker, in relation to your own experience, is what you're looking for. How much gardening has that person done, what kinds of plants has he or she grown? There's no point in trying to define what constitutes a novice gardener, or how many years and number of species grown makes someone an expert. As the designer, your own maintenance skills and ability are always going to be the benchmark. You need to know whether the caretaker has less, the same, or more experience than you do.

When you are designing your own garden and plan to maintain it yourself, you have the perfect situation. You know exactly how much you know. As you design you can ask yourself, "Will I be able to handle taking care of this plant? Will I be able to reach that spot from the path to weed it?"

While you are designing a garden to be maintained by another person, you will still look at each plant and planting arrangement and decide whether you could handle the situation. Then you must go a step further. You can allow things into the garden that you could handle if you have judged the caretaker to be equal to or beyond you in gardening skill. You will have to veto some elements for the less experienced caretaker because they require a skill you only recently mastered.

If every garden requires some maintenance, what qualifies a bed as low maintenance? Some wise person once said that in a garden the only low maintenance is the work you do while on your knees. It's a good reminder that terms such as "low" are relative. Even when the tasks to be done are well within a gardener's experience level, one

The "No-Maintenance" Garden

Don't let wishful thinking lead you to believe that you can design a garden requiring so little maintenance that the caretaker becomes unimportant. The "low-maintenance garden" is a much-sought prize, but careful shoppers will notice that this attractive selling feature brags of "low" rather than "no" maintenance. People who have asked me, seriously, to design a no-maintenance garden are the people I have advised to plant silk flowers.

hour a day spent tending the garden may be a breeze for one person, oppressive for another. That's why you have to pin down a second important fact about the designated caretaker — available time.

HOURS IN THE GARDEN

How many hours do you intend to spend each week taking care of this garden? For some people, this means deciding how many hours they can afford to give or can persuade their family to give to the garden. For those who will hire a gardener it means determining what kind of gardening services are available at what rates and figuring the number of hours their budget can handle.

The number of hours available for maintenance each week can predict how large the garden may be. My own records tell me that someone at my level of experience, working to my own standards, can take care of 300 to 400 square feet of established garden in an hour a week. You can use my figures as a starting point, but it's even better to develop your own.

Developing your own time standard means you'll have to think back about gardening you've done before or begin to track what you do in a given area this growing season. Take the hours you spend in a well-prepared new bed or an established bed during a whole season. Divide that by the number of weeks your gardening season covers to get your own personal average for maintenance

hours required per week in that size garden. Now, just as your own gardening experience is a benchmark for the kind of maintenance tasks you can include, your time standard serves as a measuring stick for the overall maintenance time required.

Once again, if you are designing gardens for yourself, figuring the time required to maintain them is a breeze. So long as you use the same means to maintain the new gardens as you did for the old, you'll be able to use your time standard and closely predict what the cost will be in hours of work. Whether you're the caretaker or you add the job to the duties of your current garden helper, it's all the same.

What about designing a garden for someone else? You need to think about neatness and efficiency to apply your time standard to someone else's garden.

Neat or not? The neatness issue can cause major differences in maintenance time required. Was your time standard based on a garden that is neater than the one you're designing should be? A certain degree of neatness comes from choice of plants. Like people, some plants operate on an even keel and are always presentable. Other plants are more moody — fairy tale princesses one month and scruffy urchins the next. Yet even when the garden is composed entirely of the most reliably presentable plants, it can be tidied up beyond its natural state. That garden composed entirely of naturally presentable plants

List the time you spend on new and established beds to determine your personal time standard:

might require 1 hour a week to live up to my standard: Naturalized is wonderful. It will probably take 2 hours a week to satisfy the person who prefers picture perfect. So, decide on a level of neatness before you estimate the amount of time that will be needed to keep the garden at that level.

Fast or slow? Then there's the efficiency question. Does the proposed caretaker work at the same speed as the caretaker who set your time standard? The comparison tells you whether to use your time standard as is or to adjust it up or down.

All you can do is guess, unless you have watched the proposed caretaker work. My guess is often based on that person's walking pace. When walking, people fall naturally into their own personal gait: Some amble, some stroll, and some march. In other words, some walk fast, some slow.

People often garden at a speed that matches their own walking gait. Don't expect an ambler to live up to a marcher's standard.

Designing for Ability

Design to meet the caretaker's current abilities. The first year in a garden's life is what counts. Its first-year rating determines whether it will live to be two years old. So, imagine a situation in which you and the caretaker seem to be a match, except that you are more experienced. You feel that eventually the caretaker will be able to take care of the garden in the same amount of time you would spend. Still, plan for that caretaker to get a little less done than you would in the same amount of time. The garden will be well tended that important first year, and the caretaker will be happy. Next year the caretaker will be more experienced and may spend even less time than you figured in the garden. Still another feather in your cap!

THE HIRED CARETAKER

You may plan to have a landscaping firm assume the care of your plantings. In that case, unless you are familiar with the firm that will be providing the services, plan for an ambler with little experience. Every firm probably has its marchers, strollers, and amblers. Planning for the garden to be maintained by a low-production, low-experience gardener increases the likelihood that any firm chosen will be able to handle the job and that any difference between planned maintenance time and actual time will be a savings rather than an added expense.

Now you have some specific information to help you match the garden to the caretaker. Add it to your list.

As we go on, I'll point out some features of a garden that increase the maintenance time, others that save time. It's up to you to make the choices for your caretaker. Your garden's life expectancy increases each time you do.

◀ At this point in the design process, your notes may look like this. Reasons for the garden, a budget, and a description of the caretaker have been established.

The Garden Owner Wants:
- variety
- color all season
- to attract hummingbirds and butterflies
- cut flowers
- to enjoy watching things grow

Budget:
- limited funds, $150 this year
- owner will do work
- must be able to be installed over 3–5 years

Caretaker:
- owner will maintain
- has some experience, not as much as I do
- enjoys garden work, Saturday mornings
- neat but tolerates a little disorder

Assess the Site

The fourth step in successful landscape design is to assess the site to determine what the site has to offer the viewer, and what plants may thrive there. The site assessment must include hours of sunlight, type of soil, availability of water, and other factors. Further along in this chapter I will provide you with the tools you need to make an accurate site assessment.

Patience Pays Off

It may have been difficult for you to complete the first three steps in the design process because your head was full of questions about the soil and sprinkler systems. Most gardeners want to get out into the garden site right away. Literally, that's familiar turf! But when designers rush right out into the yard, two unfortunate consequences may result. First, the people who were bypassed in the rush out to the yard may feel that their own wishes are not being given proper respect. The first impression is indeed important, setting the tone for an entire relationship. Do you want to assure your family or your customers that the garden is for their enjoy-

ment? Then let them hear that from you before they see a tape measure laid out across their favorite patch of lawn. Second, if the growing conditions are your first order of business, that order may never change. The resulting garden may well be a haven for plants but a disappointment for the people who wanted it. You'll be glad you waited until now to venture out into the garden-to-be.

Don't get me wrong. The most enduring gardens are those that are full of happy plants. "Right plant, right place" is my abiding philosophy. But my definition of "right" demands that the plant suit people-oriented criteria as well as environmental factors. The right plant must do what this person wants and grow happily in this place.

Establish the Main Viewpoint

Completing this step of the design process means assessing a specific site. You must identify one or more spots as likely areas for the garden. Any place you choose to put a garden is the right place if it makes sense in light of your garden

List the various spots from where the garden will be seen, then decide on a main viewpoint:

List both positive and negative features seen from the main viewpoint:

_____

_____

_____

_____

_____

_____

_____

_____

_____

_____

_____

_____

_____

_____

_____

_____

_____

_____

_____

_____

_____

_____

_____

_____

goals. The key to identifying good locations and choosing among the possibilities is to establish a main viewpoint.

People are the underlying reason for gardens. Where are the people who want this garden most likely to be found? Do they want to see the garden from that spot? If the gardener wants to attract birds to this garden and then watch those birds, any place birds can find it and the gardener can see is a suitable place. If the garden is meant to help you shake off stress, find the places you are most likely to see when you are stressed. If there are several, maybe the spot that can be seen first when getting home from work or the one that can be seen from an easy chair is best.

VISUALIZE CHANGES

It's fairly simple to figure out from where the garden will be seen. We get into trouble visualizing changes in the scenery and predicting the overall effect. Take the case of "pretty" as a goal for the garden. The designer may have a dozen highly visible spots from which to choose. Finding the place where a garden will look prettiest requires putting yourself in the shoes of the main viewer and altering the view. Although this isn't the time to focus on details of the garden's appearance, it is essential to envision general alterations. Let's spend a little time on picturing changes in a scene.

First, put yourself mentally or physically into the main viewpoint, the spot from which the garden will most often be seen. That may be the foot of the driveway, if you're looking to improve the front entrance, and you see the front door most often from the car as you leave or return home. It may be inside at the kitchen window, if the garden's purpose is to brighten up the dull hours spent peeling potatoes and washing dishes.

The garden may be seen from more than one spot. Take a look from all perspectives. Decide which viewpoint is the main one. Even if two viewpoints seem to be equally important, choose one and call it the main viewpoint. This may seem arbitrary, but the designer needs it as a base throughout the whole design process. In the illustration on page 27, the yard is seen from both the patio and the indoor sitting area just a few feet from the patio. The designer has chosen one and called it the main viewpoint. I promise you it won't limit the design at all. So elect one main viewpoint. In Steps 6 through 10, you'll thank me for this.

Make some notes about what you see, both positive and negative. You can use the site checklist to make notes, or use a drawing or photograph. If you need help envisioning changes, an eagle-eye drawing or a photograph is a good tool. That also allows you to capture a great deal of information with minimal writing, the proverbial picture worth a thousand words.

MEMORY FAILS ME

These six items should be on your checklist when you look at potential sites for a garden: the overall view, hours of sunlight, type of soil, availability of water, competing plants, and exposure. Take a good look at these aspects of the site, starting with the view and working through to exposure. But don't try to commit everything to memory. Write it down.

An example of a completed checklist is on page 52. Use the blank form opposite when you assess the site. Without it, you may overlook an item that makes a big difference in choosing or placing plants. There are few things more frustrating to me than to get comfortably into Step 5 with my notes, books, and drafting equipment, only to discover that I must go back and fill in some information I missed earlier. I wish I could tell you that it won't happen to you, even with a checklist to remind you.

SITE ASSESSMENT SHEET

The view
- area is seen mainly from:_____

dominating existing features	color	shape	texture	effect

- background could be:_____
- strong lines are:_____
- overall feeling is:_____
- good location for a garden:_____

Sunlight
- hours per day of direct sun: sun (6 hrs or more)   half sun (4–6 hrs)   shade (2–4 hrs)   dense shade (0-2 hrs)
- sunny hours: 8   9   10   11   NOON   1   2   3   4   5   6   7
- seasonal differences in sun at this spot:_____

Soil
- texture: sandy   sandy loam   loam   clay loam   clay   silty loam   silt
- aeration: loose   firm   compacted
- health of existing plants: good   poor   Notes:_____
- depth of existing roots: deep   shallow   Notes:_____

Water availability
- natural water
  - blockers:_____
  - depth of water table:_____
- irrigation via
  - automatic system: spray jets   misters   soakers/bubblers   Notes:_____
  - manual system: notes:_____
- drainage: very fast   average   poor   standing water   Notes:_____
- runoff from:_____

Root competition
- garden would share root space with:_____
- existing plants that would have to be excluded:_____

Exposure
- natural: wind   extreme heat   frost
- man-made
  - recreational activities:_____   foot traffic:_____
  - pets:_____   other:_____

▲ Use this blank checklist to assess the site you are landscaping. In the following pages, you'll learn how to gather the information for each part of the form.

The items on the checklist are arranged in order of importance to the design, which is also the order in which I'll deal with them in this chapter.

The first portion of this checklist, "View," serves only as a memory jogger for me. I rarely write on that portion of the form, though I scribble all over the other parts. That's because I make most of my "View" notes on an eagle-eye drawing. (See page 26.)

Make a Sketch

One way to help you visualize the garden site is to make sketches to go along with your site assessment list. You don't have to be an artist to do this, and you don't have to draw to scale. So relax, get out some paper and pencils, and make some rough sketches of what you see.

THE FRONT VIEW

You might find it easier to picture the area as it is seen from ground level. Some important relationships, such as depth, are lost in a drawing done from this perspective, but it definitely helps in visualizing. Often designers use a com-

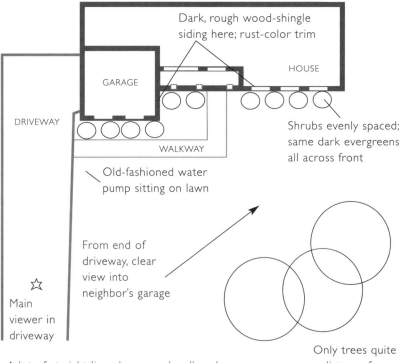

▶ Eagle-eye drawing of the house front (see page 25). Main viewpoint is at the foot of the driveway.

Dark, rough wood-shingle siding here; rust-color trim

HOUSE

GARAGE

DRIVEWAY

Shrubs evenly spaced; same dark evergreens all across front

WALKWAY

Old-fashioned water pump sitting on lawn

☆

Main viewer in driveway

From end of driveway, clear view into neighbor's garage

A lot of straight lines: house and walk, columns on porch, line of shrubs; formal feeling, quite spare

Only trees quite a distance from house

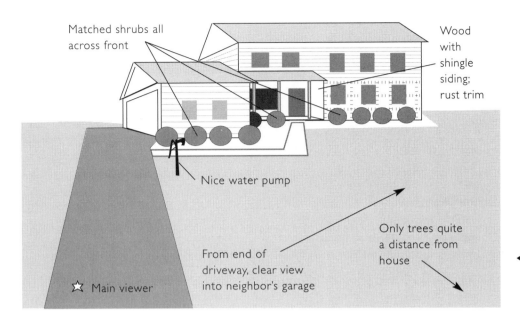

Matched shrubs all across front

Wood with shingle siding; rust trim

Nice water pump

From end of driveway, clear view into neighbor's garage

Only trees quite a distance from house

☆ Main viewer

◀ Here is the same view of the house front, but this time, it is from ground level.

bination of front view and eagle-eye drawings or photos to imagine changes. In later stages, when it can be useful to examine different viewer angles and close-up versus far view, the eagle-eye drawing becomes more important.

PICTURE THIS

If you are not able to make a front view sketch, take a photograph from the main viewpoint. You can mark ideas directly on the photograph or on a transparent overlay.

Take extra pictures or make copies to give yourself leeway to experiment. On a standard office copier, you can make copies of the photograph that are clear enough for this use. The best copies come from black and white photos. The size of the original photo shouldn't limit you. Most office copiers can enlarge the image or produce a copy on transparent film, which can then be projected and traced onto huge easel paper.

RECORD ALL THE FEATURES

Whether you are making a sketch of the site or taking photographs, it is important to include all the features that now exist at the site. Don't overlook the following:

- Buildings such as sheds or detached garages
- Trees
- Shrubs
- Plants
- Fences
- Patios and decks
- Walkways and driveways
- Other permanent features, such as utility boxes or well pipes

THE EAGLE-EYE DRAWING

You might use what I call an eagle-eye drawing to record what you see. Most designers call this a plan view. On it, the site is drawn as if you were looking down from the sky. All the important features you notice are shown on the eagle-eye, in rough relationship to each other. It's not necessary to draw to scale. Some sample eagle-eye drawings are reproduced here to help you zero in on important characteristics on the checklist: main viewing point; location of important features; shapes, textures, and colors of existing shrubs, trees, and man-made structures; lines and patterns formed by walkways and structures; the feeling you get from the existing view.

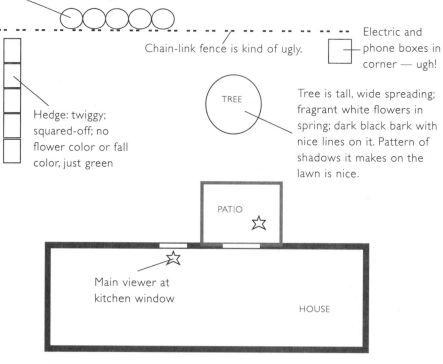

▲ This garden is meant to liven up the backyard. The main viewpoint is inside, at the kitchen window, indicated by a star. The area will also be seen from the patio. Notes record the designer's impressions when viewing the yard from the kitchen window.

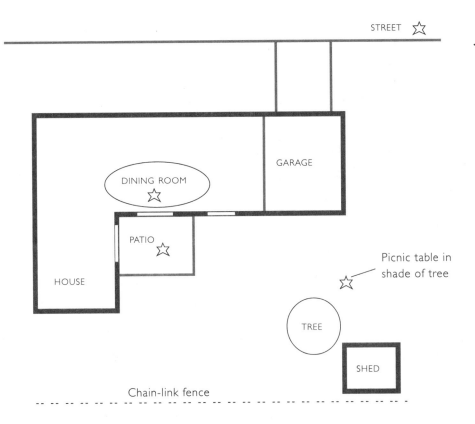

STREET ☆

GARAGE

DINING ROOM ☆

PATIO ☆

HOUSE

Picnic table in shade of tree

☆

TREE

SHED

Chain-link fence

◀ Another eagle-eye drawing of the same backyard. Here, stars identify the places from which the backyard is seen: the street, the dining room, the patio, the picnic table out in the yard. Since the yard will most often be seen from the dining area, that is designated as the main viewing point.

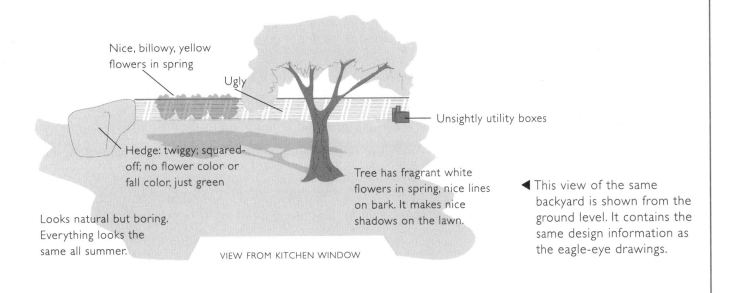

Nice, billowy, yellow flowers in spring

Ugly

Unsightly utility boxes

Hedge: twiggy; squared-off; no flower color or fall color, just green

Tree has fragrant white flowers in spring, nice lines on bark. It makes nice shadows on the lawn.

Looks natural but boring. Everything looks the same all summer.

VIEW FROM KITCHEN WINDOW

◀ This view of the same backyard is shown from the ground level. It contains the same design information as the eagle-eye drawings.

Understanding Focal Points

Select one or more likely spots for a garden, based on your assessment of the view. The concept of focal points is key to this process. Focal points are places that draw your eye, that cause you to focus for a moment during a visual sweep of a scene, that even orient you in that direction. To where is the main viewer's eye drawn? Is that focal point an attractive feature? Do the existing focal points or anything else in the situation cause viewers to orient themselves in a certain direction? Can the garden be placed to capitalize on the existing high points and orientation in the view?

Objects that are a distinctive color or shape in their setting are often focal points: a red-leaf Japanese maple in an otherwise green yard; the narrow form of a columnar oak or slender statue among rounded shrubs; a single tree in a flat carpet of lawn.

Where visual lines intersect, strong focal points result. Our eyes follow lines, literally. Where a line ends at a second line, our gaze changes direction. For a moment, our eye rests at the spot where the lines meet. Think about how your eye is drawn to the spot where the walkway intersects the front porch step; where the fence meets the horizon; where a path disappears around a row of shrubs.

Unfortunately, there are both desirable and undesirable focal points. The neighbor's swimming pool slide, jutting above the line of your fence rail, may be an annoying focal point. Then there are those hated utility pedestals above buried wires. As the only vertical elements in a horizontal sea of green, of course they stand out.

BORING VERSUS BUSY

There may be few or many focal points in a scene. We usually call it boring when there are too few focal points, busy when there are too many. The

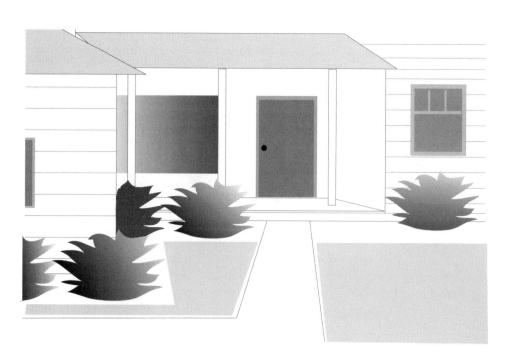

▶ The front door is an important focal point. The walkway is a strong line that leads the eye.

front of the house may be boring if it has colors and patterns that are too homogeneous and offer no distinctive place for the eye to rest. A yard may appear busy if it has too many statues or unique plants dotted about.

Make a note of the good and bad places that draw your eye as you stand in or picture the scene from the main viewpoint.

▲ Where visual lines intersect, strong focal points result, as here, where a fence meets the horizon.

▼ Likewise, a strong focal point is found where a path disappears around a row of shrubs.

LANDSCAPER'S NOTEBOOK

Assessing the Site — the View. Now that you have some sketches of the existing site, you can begin to fill out the Site Assessment Sheet. At the right is a copy of the entire form, with "The view" portion highlighted. Below is a sample of a completed form, and at the bottom is a blank for your notes.

SAMPLE:

The view

■ area is seen mainly from: _from street, the end of the driveway, and from the front door and living room_

dominating existing features	color	shape	texture	effect
house	tan & cream	boxy	medium	spotted brick, plain, unadorned
evergreen shrubs at house	deep green	clipped round	fine	dark, repetitious blobs
sidewalk to front door	very white	L-shaped	fine	beeline to front door
3 crabapple trees	white flowers	mushroomy	medium	nice, but not really part of house front, too far away
antique water pump	black iron	vertical	coarse	gets lots of attention

■ background could be: _the house, the shrubs along the front_
■ strong lines are: _the sidewalk, the vertical columns on the porch, the pump upright like a statue_
■ overall feeling is: _formal, practical_
■ good location for a garden: _Around the pump? Along the front of the house and shrubs? Near trees?_

- -

YOUR COPY:

The view

■ area is seen mainly from:_____

dominating existing features	color	shape	texture	effect

■ background could be:_____
■ strong lines are:_____
■ overall feeling is:_____
■ good location for a garden:_____

Facing Facts

We tend to square ourselves off to points of visual interest. The person standing at the kitchen window may look primarily to the northeast because a bench in that part of the yard is a strong focal point. The chairs on the patio may be angled toward the bird feeders.

We also tend to orient ourselves to the center of things. While traveling by car, you may come to places called scenic turnouts. Drivers park, get out, and stretch while enjoying a beautiful view. The site you are assessing may have something in common with many scenic turnouts: They may both be situated so that the viewer feels he or she is at the center of a wide panorama. The viewer can enjoy the scenery without any annoying sights at the periphery of his or her vision. Like sitting with your back in a corner, you have the widest possible view. From the main viewpoint, does such a spot present itself? A main viewer on a patio will probably not face the wall of the house but the larger view that presents itself in the backyard. In the eagle-eye drawing below, there is a wall running to the south and a fence running to the east. The main viewer has a wide, unbroken view to the southeast.

CAPITALIZE ON THE VIEW

Here are three ways to use what is in view to decide on a garden spot. Keep in mind that the exact location of the garden and how much ground it will cover are not important yet. What you're doing is selecting the general location.

What does the main viewer see?

_____
_____
_____
_____
_____
_____
_____
_____
_____
_____
_____
_____
_____
_____
_____
_____

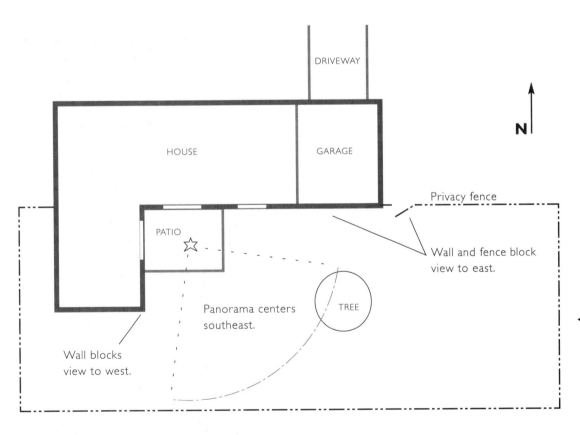

DRIVEWAY

HOUSE

GARAGE

N

Privacy fence

PATIO

Wall and fence block view to east.

Panorama centers southeast.

TREE

Wall blocks view to west.

◄ Eagle-eye drawing shows that the main viewer has an uninterrupted view when facing southeast.

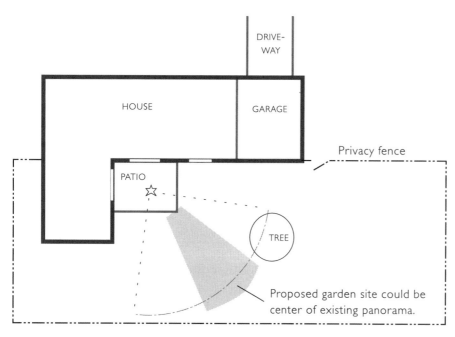

▲ The garden can be placed to take advantage of the panoramic angle . . .

Take advantage of a panoramic angle in selecting a spot for your garden. In the illustration at the top left, center stage is due southeast of the viewer. So a garden centered in that panorama, whether close to or far from the viewer, would bask in the attention already directed that way. If a distinct panorama doesn't already exist or the view is too wide open, you may choose to make one. This might be done by walling off the view in one or more directions with hedges, fences, or other structures. The garden can be planned at center stage in the resulting panorama.

Piggyback the garden on an existing, desirable focal point. If something in the view is eye catching, you might put a garden around or near it. It might even be mandated that the garden must go in the vicinity of such an eye-catcher, as when its reason for being is to dress up a statue. Even in that case, there are design choices to make. Such a garden should be placed so that someone at the main viewpoint will see it as embracing, but not obscuring, that focal point.

In the illustration at the bottom left, the designer wants to add color to the front yard and does not have to stick with decorating any specific feature. The most obvious places to use to meet this need are the area near an old-fashioned water pump and inside the bend of the front walkway. The water pump is notable because it appears to be a sculpture in the otherwise unbroken lawn. The area enclosed by the front walkway attracts the viewer's gaze because so many strong lines intersect there: walkway, porch, door, walls.

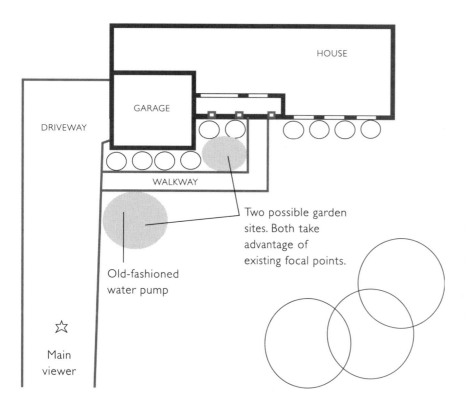

▲ . . . Or, two gardens can be placed to augment existing, desirable focal points.

Create a new focal point. Perhaps it seems like a good idea to cause the viewer to turn his or her head a different way. The viewers in the drawings below were facing a rather dreary sight and are going to be coaxed to change their ways via garden design. It's not unusual for people to unconsciously angle their chairs toward something distinctive in a scene, even if it's the utility pedestals as shown. Instead of trying to hide the utilities, the garden design at the bottom right is intended to pull the eye off to another area entirely. A trellis helps create a panoramic angle that excludes the pedestals.

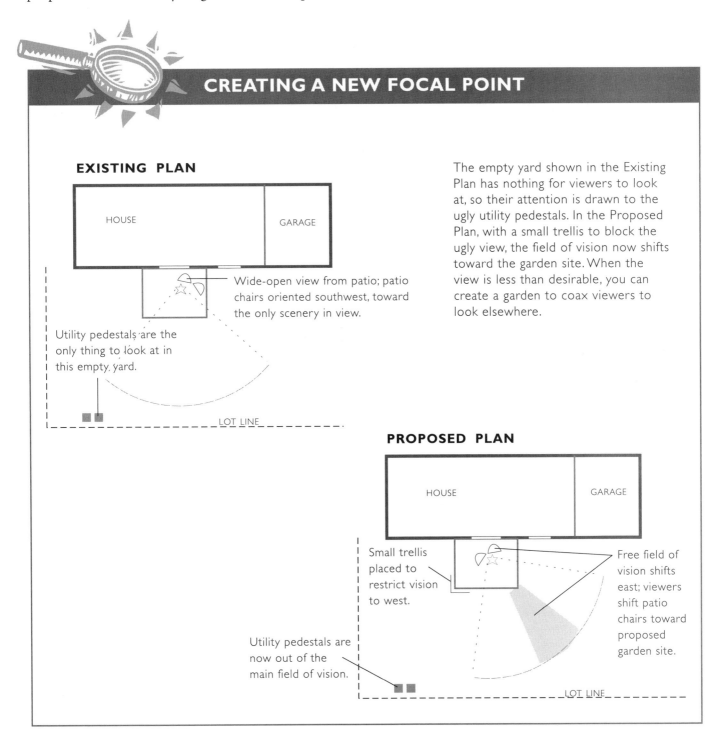

CREATING A NEW FOCAL POINT

EXISTING PLAN

HOUSE

GARAGE

Wide-open view from patio; patio chairs oriented southwest, toward the only scenery in view.

Utility pedestals are the only thing to look at in this empty yard.

LOT LINE

The empty yard shown in the Existing Plan has nothing for viewers to look at, so their attention is drawn to the ugly utility pedestals. In the Proposed Plan, with a small trellis to block the ugly view, the field of vision now shifts toward the garden site. When the view is less than desirable, you can create a garden to coax viewers to look elsewhere.

PROPOSED PLAN

HOUSE

GARAGE

Small trellis placed to restrict vision to west.

Free field of vision shifts east; viewers shift patio chairs toward proposed garden site.

Utility pedestals are now out of the main field of vision.

LOT LINE

All for One and One for All

There are times when there is more than one viewer, and even though you've dubbed one as "main," you want to check now to make sure that the garden site will make everyone happy. The most logical spot for your garden in this case may be an area that can be seen by all the viewers you've identified. An eagle-eye drawing, done to scale, is most helpful for identifying such a spot. On it, you can mark the edges of each viewer's field of vision and connect those spots to the appropriate viewers. You may discover an area of overlap, like the one shown in the illustration below.

The cone-shaped lines radiating from each viewpoint represent that viewer's comfortable field of vision. There is no good equation to help you predict a particular viewer's field of vision: The amount of space comfortably seen without turning the head varies with the people and the circumstances. Someone standing on a deck, well away from any building, large trees, or shrubs may be considered to have a field of vision greater than 180°. With a tree to one side, that same viewer may sense the obstruction and unconsciously narrow his or her scope quite dramatically. When a notable object is situated a short distance in front of the viewer, a separate close field of vision, narrower in scope and shorter in focus, may result. From within a house, the field of vision

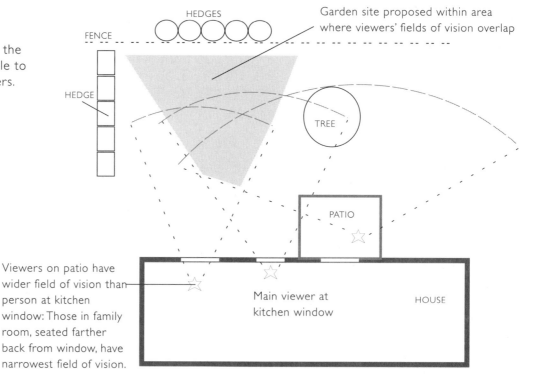

▶ If possible, situate the garden to be visible to all potential viewers.

HEDGES

Garden site proposed within area where viewers' fields of vision overlap

FENCE

HEDGE

TREE

PATIO

Viewers on patio have wider field of vision than person at kitchen window: Those in family room, seated farther back from window, have narrowest field of vision.

Main viewer at kitchen window

HOUSE

is restricted by both the width of the window or door in front of you and your distance from that door. Make some observations of your own in various yards and from different apertures to give you a feel for using the field of vision cones you'll encounter throughout this book.

Without a scale drawing, resign yourself to a bit more legwork when looking for that overlap. Go to the first viewpoint and mentally note whatever marks the edges of your comfortable field of vision. It may be wise to go out in the yard and place a marker of some sort at each edge. Then move to the next viewpoint and note the areas, if any, that were in your first field of vision and are still easy to see. Continue moving among the viewpoints until you have identified one or more locations that could be enjoyed by all your viewers.

RULES MEANT TO BE BROKEN

Here are some other thoughts to consider as you select potential garden sites. If any of these sound like rules, then this is a good time to learn the one rule of gardening: Every rule can be beautifully broken. Like this garden design process, all garden rules are just launching pads.

Distant gardens must be large. The farther the garden is from the main viewer, the larger it must be to get its fair share of the limelight. The yardstick I use says that the garden should have some aspect that has a visual dimension at least half as large as the distance between viewer and garden. So a garden

40 feet away from the main viewpoint would be about 20 feet across. It could also be 20 feet tall, but not many gardens can measure up in that way. Brightness comes into play as well and can compensate somewhat for small size, but we'll deal with that a little later in design. At this point, let's agree that most large gardens require large investments in time and money and that distant gardens require large budgets.

Gardens draw attention. Trying to hide an eyesore behind a garden is a bit like dressing in red sequined clothing when you want to keep a low profile at a business event. Try to avoid using a garden to screen out the neighbor's garbage cans or a utility pedestal. While the garden is young and during part of the year, it may not hide the eyesore so much as call extra attention to it. Use a group of large shrubs or a fence as a visual barrier, something that has more immediate screening ability and more year-round effectiveness than a garden. You may even find that once you've blocked off the offending view, that particular area is not your first choice as a focal point. If it is still the place you want to garden, you can build a showy garden in front of the shrubs or fencing.

Small gardens make good screens. If you must focus your gardening efforts on hiding an eyesore, stop for a moment and hold your hand straight up, palm out, in front of your face. Notice that this relatively small object can block out a large portion of the horizon. In this way you can see that it's not necessary to plant a large garden right up against an eyesore to hide it. A comparatively small garden closer to the main viewer can serve the same purpose.

Note the field of vision at each viewpoint:

View A
_____
_____
_____
_____
_____

View B
_____
_____
_____
_____
_____

View C
_____
_____
_____
_____
_____

View D
_____
_____
_____
_____
_____

Unique Conditions: What Can Defeat a Garden?

What I call unique conditions are miscellaneous features of a site that require gardeners to spend exorbitant amounts of time and money to get a garden growing. Like combinations on a slot machine, these kinds of conditions may be unremarkable by themselves, but when they appear in certain locations they can make you jump up and down and stamp your feet. Some can be predicted as you look over the site. Where they exist, you are advised either to choose a different spot or accept an increase in your budget. Chief among unique conditions that bother gardeners: buried debris, buried utility pipe, and wires; difficult access to the garden site that requires all material to be wheelbarrowed in through an obstacle course; and other people working in the area at the same time, particularly those who wield spray equipment and power tools or drive heavy machinery.

Looking Out from the Plants' Perspective

Now you can assess the growing conditions at each potential garden site. Up until now you've been thinking and looking from a human viewpoint. Now take the point of view of a plant as you look at each likely spot for the garden. The most beautiful gardens are those with healthy, lush plants. The information you gather now will help you find plants that will thrive in your garden. The rest of this chapter is a guide to determining what your plants will have to live with in terms of the amount of sunlight, type of soil, availability of water, competition from other plants, and exposure to miscellaneous elements.

SUNLIGHT IS CRITICAL

First, determine how many hours of sun there are each day at the spot you're assessing. You can circle the appropriate sunlight category on the checklist and note any differences in sunlight at various times of the day or year.

The amount of direct sunlight that is available each day is a critical factor when it comes to plant health. Compare a plant in an incompatible light situation to a person who has a bad case of the flu. First the person slows down, then puts aside nonessential activities. As the sickness continues and energies continue to be drained by the flu, the person may be more likely to contract a cold or other infection. Plants are not much different. When stressed, they don't flower as well, grow more slowly or stop growing, and become easier targets for diseases and insects.

Assessing the Site — Sunlight. Use this part of the Site Assessment Sheet to record both the total number of hours of sun the site receives and the specific hours of sunlight. Note any special conditions, such as seasonal differences caused by the sun's angle or tree foliage.

SITE ASSESSMENT SHEET

The view
- area is seen mainly from:_____

dominating existing features	color	shape	texture	effect

- background could be:_____
- strong lines are:_____
- overall feeling is:_____
- good location for a garden:_____

Sunlight
- hours per day of direct sun: sun (6 hrs or more) half sun (4–6 hrs) shade (2–4 hrs) dense shade (0-2 hrs)
- sunny hours: 8 9 10 11 NOON 1 2 3 4 5 6 7
- seasonal differences in sun at this spot:_____

Soil
- texture: sandy sandy loam loam clay loam clay silty loam silt
- aeration: loose firm compacted
- health of existing plants: good poor Notes:_____
- depth of existing roots: deep shallow Notes:_____

Water availability
- natural water
  - blockers:_____
  - depth of water table:_____
- irrigation via
  - automatic system: spray jets misters soakers/bubblers Notes:_____
  - manual system: Notes:_____
- drainage: very fast average poor standing water Notes:_____
- runoff from:_____

Root competition
- garden would share root space with:_____
- existing plants that would have to be excluded:_____

Exposure
- natural: wind extreme heat frost
- man-made
  - recreational activities:_____ foot traffic:_____
  - pets:_____ other:_____

SAMPLE:

Sunlight

But full sun farther away from the house and shade under the crabapples

- hours per day of direct sun: sun (6 hrs or more)   (half sun (4–6 hrs))   shade (2–4 hrs)   dense shade (0-2 hrs)
- sunny hours: (8 9 10 11 NOON) 1 2 3 4 5 6 7
- seasonal differences in sun at this spot: _None by the house; it blocks the sun all year. Shady area near_ _tree. Changes to full sun when there are no leaves._

- -

YOUR COPY:

Sunlight

- hours per day of direct sun: sun (6 hrs or more)   half sun (4–6 hrs)   shade (2–4 hrs)   dense shade (0-2 hrs)
- sunny hours: 8 9 10 11 NOON 1 2 3 4 5 6 7
- seasonal differences in sun at this spot:_____

Hibiscus: A Case History

I've seen many examples of plants suffering from sunlight shortage or overdose. Some hibiscus plants are my personal reminders of sunlight's critical nature. Hardy hibiscus (*Hibiscus moscheutos*) are fabulous plants with huge, bright flowers in August. Something I read when I first started growing them said they could grow in half sun, so I put them where they received about 4 hours of sun a day. Their performance was less than spectacular in that spot. Not only were there few flowers, but the leaves were nearly skeletonized by insects. I doubted that they would survive the winter after such a bad year. But the next spring they showed signs of life, so I moved them to the full sun, about 35 feet away. They have bloomed prolifically for 10 years in this second spot and never once have their leaves been eaten. The truth is that hibiscus belong in full sun. The troublesome insects could have moved with the plants. The fact that those insects no longer prey on the plants is a testimonial to a plant's natural ability to deter pests and disease if it is healthy enough.

BRIGHTNESS VERSUS SUNLIGHT

Don't confuse sunlight with brightness of light and heat. When there is direct sunlight on a leaf, the leaf will cast a shadow. Brightness and heat can affect plant growth, but they are not a substitute for sunlight. A little later, we'll consider brightness and heat as components of "exposure." For now, concentrate on how much direct sun there is at the spot you intend to garden.

DEFINING SUN AND SHADE

We acknowledge that plants are sunlight specialists whenever we pick up a new plant in the nursery and examine the pot tag to see whether the plant prefers sun, half sun, or shade. Probably you are familiar with the symbols shown in the box on page 39. These are generally understood to mean "sunny," "part sunny," and "shady".

Unfortunately, "sunny" and "shady" are not defined on the tags and are probably misinterpreted more than any other direction for growing plants. After I had been gardening seriously for several years, my records showed that most of my experimenting, transplanting, and plant losses were related to lack of information on sunlight requirements. I decided I needed an objective way to determine whether a particular area in a garden was best described as full sun, half sun, or shade. The method I use is spelled out in the box "Says Who?" on the opposite page. In the years since I developed my method, it has served its purpose well for hundreds of gardeners and garden sites in my home area, the "thumb" area of Michigan. It will work for you if you are at about 42° north latitude. If you are farther north or south, you'll have to modify it somewhat.

I developed my definitions of "sun," "shade," and "part sun" using standard pot tags and my gardening notes on almost two hundred perennial species. Pot tags are produced by a few large companies for nurseries nationwide. The plants were species I had grown for a number of years under the try-and-see method: Plant it, watch it, compare it to the size and appearance described for the species in textbooks, move it if it doesn't measure up. Initially, it would take several years to find the right spot for a

plant using this method. Eventually, I accelerated the try-and-see method by starting with three or more individuals of the same species so that I could evaluate the plant's performance in several different places within a single growing season.

I located each plant in the nursery and recorded its sunlight symbol from the pot tag. What this did was indicate certain areas in my garden that must be "sunny" by the pot tag definition, since the majority of species that had grown well in those areas had "sun" tags at the nursery.

There were discrepancies between my records and some of the pot tags, but not a large number, so I disregarded them. (More on that in the next chapter.)

Then I went to the spots my plants and the pot tags agreed were "sunny" and recorded how many hours of sun reached that spot each day during the height of the growing season. From this came my findings: "Sun" means more than 6 hours of direct sunlight each day.

Sun	Part Sun	Shade

HYBRID DAYLILY PERENNIAL

Trumpet shaped flowers on tall stalks in summer. Attractive foliage. HOW TO GROW: Plant in sun or part shade, 18 in. apart. Grows to 36" tall depending on variety.

BLUE COLUMBINE AQUILEGIA PERENNIAL

Pale blue and white flowers atop lacy foliage. Use in borders, beds. HOW TO GROW: Plant in sun or part shade, 18 in. apart. Grows to 36" tall depending on variety.

WHITE-EDGE HOSTA PERENNIAL

Striking foliage. Lilac bell flowers on tall stalks in late summer. HOW TO GROW: Plant in full or part shade, 18 in. apart. Grows to 24" tall depending on variety.

◄ Pot tags like these can help you choose plants at the nursery. But you should first understand the definitions of "sun," "half sun," and "shade."

About "shade-tolerant" plants: Many plants that love sun die in the shade. Shade-tolerant plants grow best in sun or half sun but will continue to grow if conditions become shadier after the plants mature. Flowering and growth rates generally decrease as shade increases.

IS YOUR GARDEN SUNNY, HALF SUNNY, OR SHADY?

The key to successful landscaping is determining how many hours of sun the garden receives each day during the growing season. If you are planning your garden in the off-season or on a cloudy day, it may be difficult to judge how much sunlight reaches a given spot. A site that is sunny all summer may be shady in winter. The shadows on the site in the winter are there because the sun has "moved" on the horizon. Follow these six steps to figure out the amount of sun the garden will get in the summer, no matter when you do your site assessment. (Sunrise and sunset locations and seasonal elevations here are plotted for southern Michigan. Farther south in the United States there is less difference between winter and summer sun locations; farther north, there is more difference.)

STEP 1.
STAND IN THE CENTER OF THE SITE, FACING DUE SOUTH.

■ You can use a map to find south,

or

■ Face the noon sun. At true noon (not daylight saving time noon!), if you face south your shadow is directly behind you.

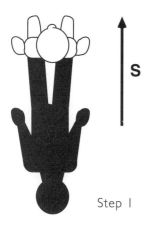

Step 1

STEP 2.
FIND WHERE THE SUN RISES AND SETS ON THE HORIZON IN SUMMER.
The sun doesn't rise due east and set due west every day of the year.

■ Imagine the ground around you is a clock, lying flat on the ground, face up. You're standing at the center. Noon (12) on the clock is due south.

■ Picture the minute hand of that clock marking the hours of sunrise and sunset at different seasons of the year:

Spring (Mar. 21) and **fall** (Sept. 21): sunrise at quarter to the hour; sunset at quarter after

Summer (June 22): sunrise at 19 minutes to the hour; sunset at 19 minutes after the hour

Winter (Dec. 22): sunrise at 12 minutes to the hour; sunset at 12 minutes after the hour

■ Notice that an object at the # symbol will cast a shadow toward the center of the clock just before sunset in winter, but not in summer.

STEP 3.
NOTICE WHAT BLOCKS THE MORNING OR EVENING SUN.
Looking toward the summer sunrise and sunset locations, you can see whether anything will block the sunlight early and late in the day.

■ Objects close to you will block the sun for a longer period of time than objects farther away.

■ Tall objects block the sun longer than short objects.

■ Don't be fooled by leafless tree branches. A tree is very good at what it does; that is, it will grow a leaf into every available patch of

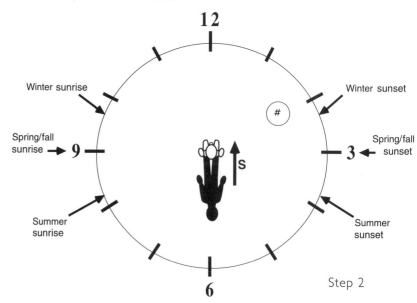

Step 2

sun. If there are branches between you and the sun, there will be some shade.

STEP 4.

Now look for what might block the midday sun.

Look toward the midday summer sun. Don't use the winter midday sun as your guide. The sun is much higher in the midday sky in summer than in winter, so north-side shadows are much shorter in summer. The 6-foot-deep bed along the north side of your house may be completely shaded at noon in December, but only the 2 feet closest to the building will be shaded in June. Again, an imaginary clock can help you map the sun's course, this time to determine where in the sky the sun will be at noon on a summer day.

■ Imagine there is a clock standing up alongside you:
  12 on the clock face is directly above your head.
  Quarter after the hour (3) is lined up due south on the horizon.

■ Picture the minute hand:
  In winter, the noon sun is low, at 11 minutes after the hour.
  In spring and fall, the noon sun is at 7 minutes after the hour.
  In summer, the noon (1 p.m. daylight saving time) sun is at 3 minutes after the hour.

STEP 5.

Map the sun's path in summer. Estimate the number of hours you will be able to see the sun.

Point at the spot where the sun will rise, then swing your arm in an arc along the sun's path through its noon location and over to the spot where it will set. Note all the unobstructed sections along that path. Those are the sunny hours.

■ Add up the hours you will be able to see the summer sun from this spot. Figure that the sun makes it halfway up from the horizon toward its noon position by 9 A.M., halfway from noon to sunset by 3 P.M.

■ Note the time(s) of day there will be shade. Some shade during the hottest part of the day can be a plus. Spots that are in shade all morning, where dew remains for hours on plants, can be a problem. Fungus and some bacteria thrive in cool, moist locations like this.

STEP 6.

Label your spot according to the hours of direct sun it receives.

Sun = 6 or more hours of sun each day

Half sun (half shade) = 4 to 6 hours of sun each day

Shade = 2 to 4 hours of sun each day

Dense shade = 0 to 2 hours of sun each day

Summer shade = full sun in spring (end of May), shade to dense shade in summer. Also called "filtered sun."

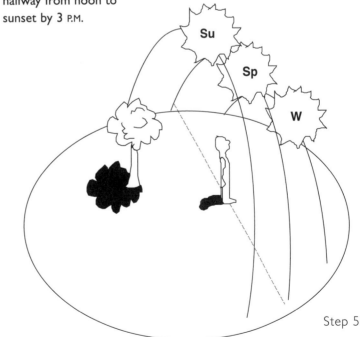

Step 5

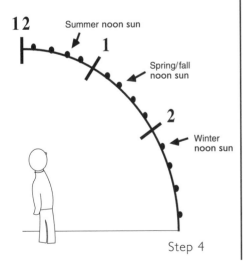

Step 4

Use definitive hours. Since the time I developed these numbers, I have found references that use the definitive hours per day to describe sunlight requirements. In comparing references that use the definitive hours per day to those that use the less precise "sun," "shade," etc. on nursery pot tags, I have been pleased to see my findings supported. So it's worth the time to map the sun and pinpoint the number of hours of sun per day in a specific place in your yard. It's a figure that you can use with any reference you may have.

SOIL SUPPORT FOR YOUR PLANTS

Once you know how much sun there will be in a spot, make some notes about the soil. Soil is essential to plant growth, both as an anchor and because it holds nutrients and water. But all soils are not created equal. Some soils are too loose or shallow to be a good anchor; others hold too much water or too few nutrients. Some plants have adapted to living with particular types of soil, while others can adapt to a wide range of soil conditions. It's not necessary here to go into how each soil type behaves and which plants are adapted to which soils. What is important is that you recognize what type of soil you have and accept the fact that it cannot be changed greatly — only modified to a certain extent. With this information in hand, you can decide whether you will garden in that soil and then select plants that will grow in it.

The main thing you need to know is what type of soil texture exists where the garden might be: sand, silt, clay, or loam. Most soils have some amounts of large, coarse mineral particles (sand), fine mineral particles (silt), very fine mineral particles (clay), and decomposed organic material (humus). What we call the soil and how it behaves depends on how much of each component there is in your soil. Sandy soils consist mostly of sand particles, silty soils of silt particles, clay soils of clay particles, and loams are an intermediate mix of different particles and humus. You have two options to determine your soil texture: to have the soil tested or to test it yourself.

HOMESTYLE SOIL TESTS

To test the soil yourself, feel it or make a solution of it.

Test by feel. Take a handful of soil from the area you're considering for the garden. Take it from where you want your garden plants' roots to grow: below that thin layer of topsoil that was spread when the lawn was first established. It

Send It to the Lab

Most state Cooperative Extension Services offer inexpensive, reliable soil tests through local agricultural colleges. To use this service, take several samples of soil to a depth of several inches below the surface throughout an area, and send a composite sample in a small box to the soil-testing laboratory. They will mail the results back to you. In my state, the results include not only soil texture but soil fertility level, fertilizer recommendation, and acidity or alkalinity measurement. (Any information you get in addition to soil type can be helpful but is not essential at this point.) Check with your Cooperative Extension Service to take advantage of this service.

should be moist but not dripping for this test. Rub it between your fingers.

- Sandy soil feels gritty.
- Silts are floury or slippery, not gritty like sand, not as plastic as clay.
- Clay soil is slippery and can be molded to one degree or another.
- Loam has some grit, some slipperiness, and is often quite dark; richer in color than the others.

If you have a question about what you feel, compare your soil to a known substance: Put some damp sandbox sand in one hand and your soil in another; wet some modeling clay and rub your fingers on it, then on your soil.

Home test when fingers fail. To make a solution to test your soil, fill a quart jar about ⅔ full of water. Add a teaspoon of detergent. Add enough of your soil to almost fill the jar. Leave some air space so that there is room for the water and soil to mix when you shake the jar. Shake the jar vigorously, to dissolve all the soil. Leave the jar for several hours or a day in a place where it won't be jostled. As the soil and water separate, the soil particles will sort themselves by weight. What you will see after the soil has settled are layers: heavy sand particles at the bottom of the jar, lighter silt above, and a layer of clay particles on top. (Some clay particles are so light that they will remain suspended, muddying the water, almost indefinitely.) What you would most like to see is a loam: about equal portions of sand and silt, with a smaller amount of clay.

If you want to get quite technical, you can use the proportions of sand, clay, and silt in your sample to classify it within one of 12 or more soil texture types. When 70 percent or more of the particles is sand, it's called a sandy soil. After a loam, sandy soils are my second favorite for gardening. Silt and clay soils require the most effort of the gardener.

They have somewhere between 40 percent and 80 percent silt or clay and are called by the name of the majority particle; for example, silty loam, silty clay, clay loam, and so on.

SOIL CLUES

Beyond testing for soil type, you can take some clues about soil from plants already growing on the spot you want to garden. Warning: Some sods are not good to use as indicators. Sod is something that is often kept alive via artificial life support: daily watering and frequent fertilization. A self-supporting lawn, existing shrubs, or even first-year weeds growing on recently graded soil can tell you about soil fertility, compaction, and drainage.

- Are the plants there of varied species and generally healthy? The soil is probably fertile.
- Dig into the soil and check plant roots. Do they have deep roots or shallow? Although some plants tend to grow a lot of surface roots regardless of the soil they're in, if numerous species are there and all have shallow, flattened root systems, you're looking at compacted or poorly drained soil.

COMMON MISCONCEPTIONS

A few notes about common soil misconceptions. Not all bad soils are clay. Not all clay is bad soil. Not all topsoil is good soil.

Sometimes people assure me they have clay soil. When I ask how they know they have clay, the response might be, "Because it takes a pick axe to make a hole in it," or "Because water just sits there for days after a rain." Soil of any texture can become compacted to the point where extreme effort is necessary to break it up. Any texture soil can be

Assessing the Site — Soil. This part of the Site Assessment Sheet is the spot to record information about the characteristics of your soil. Undertake one or two of the "homestyle" soil tests described on page 42 to determine the soil texture. Observe the quality of the plants that are already growing in the area — even weeds!

SITE ASSESSMENT SHEET

The view
- area is seen mainly from:_____

dominating existing features	color	shape	texture	effect

- background could be:_____
- strong lines are:_____
- overall feeling is:_____
- good location for a garden:_____

Sunlight
- hours per day of direct sun: sun (6 hrs or more) half sun (4–6 hrs) shade (2–4 hrs) dense shade (0-2 hrs)
- sunny hours: 8 9 10 11 NOON 1 2 3 4 5 6 7
- seasonal differences in sun at this spot:_____

Soil
- texture: sandy sandy loam loam clay loam clay silty loam silt
- aeration: loose firm compacted
- health of existing plants: good poor Notes:_____
- depth of existing roots: deep shallow Notes:_____

Water availability
- natural water
  - blockers:_____
  - depth of water table:_____
- irrigation via
  - automatic system: spray jets misters soakers/bubblers Notes:_____
  - manual system: Notes:_____
- drainage: very fast average poor standing water Notes:_____
- runoff from:_____

Root competition
- garden would share root space with:_____
- existing plants that would have to be excluded:_____

Exposure
- natural: wind extreme heat frost
- man-made
  - recreational activities:_____ foot traffic:_____
  - pets:_____ other:_____

SAMPLE:

Soil

- texture: sandy   sandy loam   (loam)   clay loam   clay   silty loam   silt
- aeration: loose   (firm)   compacted
- health of existing plants: (good)   poor   Notes: _Seems OK; shrubs grow fast. Crabapples have lots of sucklings._
- depth of existing roots: (deep)   shallow   Notes: _Lawn is really deep rooted; shrubs may be less so._

- -

YOUR COPY:

Soil

- texture: sandy   sandy loam   loam   clay loam   clay   silty loam   silt
- aeration: loose   firm   compacted
- health of existing plants: good   poor   Notes:_____
- depth of existing roots: deep   shallow   Notes:_____

poorly drained because of compaction, high water table, or poor grading. Most soils around homes are compacted to a certain extent. Heavy machinery and materials used to build the house sat on the soil and crushed out the air spaces, compressing the particles of humus. Years later, the soil will still be compacted unless some action is taken to aerate the soil and introduce more humus. Even if the original soil was left in place, it may have been crushed to the point where you will swear the topsoil must have been stripped, because your soil seems so different from the soil in the undisturbed field next door. So don't assume it's clay; feel it or test it.

Clay soils can actually have more nutrients available and better water retention than sand soils. What makes some clay tough for gardening is a shortage of air. Roots need air in the soil to be able to take up nutrients and to have space to grow. Some of the nicest gardens I've seen are grown on clay loam, which is clay soil that was broken up to create air spaces and has had humus added to hold the air spaces open.

All topsoil is not great soil. Topsoil, as you will find it at garden and landscape centers, is soil that has been scraped off one area to be moved into another. It may or may not have been screened to remove rocks and debris. In the process of being moved around, scooped and piled, it has been broken up and has had air mixed into it. It may be a clay, silt, sand, or loam soil. It may have been right near the surface and be alive with the beneficial organisms and nutrients that create soil fertility. On the other hand, it may have been 8 or 12 inches below the surface at the point of origin and be relatively low in soil microorganisms or nutrients.

With that, I will leave any further discussion of soil to others. Wrap up this part of your checklist and move on.

WATER IS CRUCIAL

Availability of water is the next feature you should notice. How much water is available naturally, and how much from irrigation systems? Will there be any problems with runoff or erosion or standing water?

But I Need Some Brought In!

Never assume that you can bring in topsoil and automatically improve your soil. Botanical gardens sometimes import huge amounts of topsoil, but not without testing it first. I have twice had the opportunity to test both the existing soil and the topsoil coming in to fill around a new house. Once, the topsoil being brought in was essentially the same as the existing soil; once the topsoil was much poorer than what was already there. To improve the soil, it is wisest to either bring in soil of a known quality or simply amend the existing soil with organic matter, fertilizers, and so on. In my area, landscape suppliers sell a product called "50–50 mix," which is what I use when I need additional soil for a garden. This is a mixture made at the landscape center of 50 percent peat and 50 percent screened topsoil (usually a silty loam with good organic content).

Natural water. This includes rain, snow, and groundwater. Rain and snow can be blocked and desert conditions created by buildings on the windward side, overhanging eaves, or evergreens. You'll need to provide special supplemental irrigation to make most plants grow under things that block rain and snow. Some gardeners are fortunate enough to have a high (ground) water table, maybe even a pond or lake nearby. Groundwater moves up in the soil by a process called capillary action. If the water table is within a few feet below your ground level, your garden can benefit.

Irrigation systems. These can be mixed blessings. Automatic sprinklers are great labor savers, but most of them are set up to keep lawns constantly moist. That kind of system usually makes a garden too wet. The best automatic irrigation system to serve both lawn and gardens has separate zones for the gardens. In garden zones the water is delivered via less powerful spray heads than in lawn areas, or through soaker hoses. Where garden zones can be set to water more deeply and less often than lawn zones, that's ideal.

OTHER WATER-RELATED PROBLEMS

Runoff and erosion may seem terrible to have to deal with, but standing water is probably worse.

Runoff. Note whether the area slopes and may erode once any existing turf is taken away. Possibility of runoff should prompt the designer to arrange plants in terrace fashion, so that as much water as possible is diverted to slower, transverse courses down the slope.

Standing water. This can't be taken care of simply by rearranging plants. It has to be corrected by raising the bed above the water, draining the area, or designing solely with plants that can live in oxygen-poor, flooded soils.

Sprinkling Systems Shouldn't Dampen Your Resolve

Don't think that you cannot put a garden in a spot where it will not be watered by an automatic lawn sprinkler system. It is simply another piece of information you're gathering that will help you choose and place plants for the best possible garden on this spot.

Manual watering systems are those that are dependent on the gardener, the type of sprinkler, and the length of hose available. If this is the type of irrigation the garden will have, forecast the dependability of that system while you stand in the proposed garden site. If this were your garden, right now, what would you have to go through to get a hose out to it and set a sprinkler? The idea is to be realistic, so that when you choose plants, you won't put a plant that must have consistently cool, moist soil in a place where the nearest spigot is 75 feet away and the longest available hose is 50 feet.

LANDSCAPER'S NOTEBOOK

Assessing the Site — Water Availability. Water is crucial to the success of almost every garden. Use this part of the form to note its availability, whether from rain or groundwater or from manual or automatic irrigation. Note the lay of the land as well, and write down whatever you can observe about drainage and runoff.

SITE ASSESSMENT SHEET

The view
▪ area is seen mainly from:_____

dominating existing features	color	shape	texture	effect

▪ background could be:_____
▪ strong lines are:_____
▪ overall feeling is:_____
▪ good location for a garden:_____

Sunlight
▪ hours per day of direct sun: sun (6 hrs or more) half sun (4–6 hrs) shade (2–4 hrs) dense shade (0-2 hrs)
▪ sunny hours: 8 9 10 11 NOON 1 2 3 4 5 6 7
▪ seasonal differences in sun at this spot:_____

Soil
▪ texture: sandy sandy loam loam clay loam clay silty loam silt
▪ aeration: loose firm compacted
▪ health of existing plants: good poor Notes:_____
▪ depth of existing roots: deep shallow Notes:_____

Water availability
▪ natural water
  ▪ blockers:_____
  ▪ depth of water table:_____
▪ irrigation via
  ▪ automatic system: spray jets misters soakers/bubblers Notes:_____
  ▪ manual system: Notes:_____
▪ drainage: very fast average poor standing water Notes:_____
▪ runoff from:_____

Root competition
▪ garden would share root space with:_____
▪ existing plants that would have to be excluded:_____

Exposure
▪ natural: wind extreme heat frost
▪ man-made
  recreational activities:_____ foot traffic:_____
  pets:_____ other:_____

SAMPLE:

Water availability

▪ natural water
  ▪ blockers: _Always dry right near house because of overhanging roof, garage blocking rain._
  ▪ depth of water table: _Unknown, but former owners said had really deep well._
▪ irrigation via
  ▪ automatic system: spray jets (misters) soakers/bubblers Notes: _Turn on whenever big lawn jets do._
  ▪ manual system: Notes:_____
▪ drainage: very fast (average) poor standing water Notes: _Some areas puddle up for a day after rain._
▪ runoff from: _Downspouts empty the whole roof at both ends of shrub row._

- -

YOUR COPY:

Water availability

▪ natural water
  ▪ blockers:_____
  ▪ depth of water table:_____
▪ irrigation via
  ▪ automatic system: spray jets misters soakers/bubblers Notes:_____
  ▪ manual system: Notes:_____
▪ drainage: very fast average poor standing water Notes:_____
▪ runoff from: _____

COMPETITION FROM OTHER PLANTS

Now we're into the root competition section of the checklist. Competition from other plants is a factor in a garden's success. Woody plants' roots are the chief ones to think about. Look up as you stand in the spot you're assessing. Are there tree branches overhead? Then there are probably tree roots below your feet. Tree roots extend even beyond the branches of the tree and take almost unbelievable amounts of water and nutrients from the soil. But don't let the existence of competing roots rule out the site. Although you may not be able to have some plants, such as peony, that are not very tolerant of root competition, it is possible to correct for the problem with increased water and fertilizer.

Are you familiar with the advice, "If you can't say something nice, don't say anything at all?" One competing plant, quack grass, is hard for me to be positive about. The only good thing I can find to say about that plant is that it is extremely good at what it does: invading gardens. I always note whether it looks like the lawn in this area will behave itself around a garden.

Get to the Root of the Matter

As you assess a potential garden site, be sure to make note of nearby trees. Tree roots extend beyond the tree's branches and can rob the soil of the water and nutrients your garden will need. If you are set on a site that is near trees, be prepared to put in the extra work of watering and fertilizing the garden in order to make up for what the tree roots will take for themselves.

EXPOSURE

The last feature to note as you assess the site is something of a catchall. I call it exposure to natural and man-made plant stressors: wind, frost, extreme heat, sports equipment, or heavy traffic. All of

DESIGN BASICS

Relax: Nothing's Impossible

I realize that reading through this litany of conditions can get oppressive. Sunlight, soil type, and water are the three most important elements to notice when you assess a site; root competition and exposure are less likely to make or break a garden. So this seems like a good point to take a breather and tell you that despite some of the awful things I've pointed out to you, I've found that very few spots are impossible to garden. What you do is anticipate the growing conditions and choose plants for those conditions, or modify the site. If this is your first garden, try to choose a place with these growing conditions: full or half sun, soil that drains well and has some loam in it, and a reliable irrigation system. If you can choose between several likely sites, select the one that comes closest to those conditions just listed.

LANDSCAPER'S NOTEBOOK

Assessing the Site — Root Competition. This is a variation on the theme of availability of water. Make notes on all of the other plants in the area, including trees, shrubs, lawn grasses, flower beds, and even weeds. All of these will compete for the available water and nutrients.

SITE ASSESSMENT SHEET

The view
- area is seen mainly from:_____

dominating existing features	color	shape	texture	effect

- background could be:_____
- strong lines are:_____
- overall feeling is:_____
- good location for a garden:_____

Sunlight
- hours per day of direct sun: sun (6 hrs or more) half sun (4–6 hrs) shade (2–4 hrs) dense shade (0-2 hrs)
- sunny hours: 8 9 10 11 NOON 1 2 3 4 5 6 7
- seasonal differences in sun at this spot:_____

Soil
- texture: sandy sandy loam loam clay loam clay silty loam silt
- aeration: loose firm compacted
- health of existing plants: good poor Notes:_____
- depth of existing roots: deep shallow Notes:_____

Water availability
- natural water
  - blockers:_____
  - depth of water table:_____
- irrigation via
  - automatic system: spray jets misters soakers/bubblers Notes:_____
  - manual system: Notes:_____
- drainage: very fast average poor standing water Notes:_____
- runoff from:_____

Root competition
- garden would share root space with:_____
- existing plants that would have to be excluded:_____

Exposure
- natural: wind extreme heat frost
- man-made
  - recreational activities:_____ foot traffic:_____
  - pets:_____ other:_____

SAMPLE:

Root competition

- garden would share root space with: _Nothing, unless it's out by crabapples._
- existing plants that would have to be excluded: _Lots of taller, fast-growing patches in lawn — quack grass_

- -

YOUR COPY:

Root competition

- garden would share root space with:_____
- existing plants that would have to be excluded:_____

these are conditions that you try to compensate for in your design, but none of them would be reason enough to relocate the garden:

Wind. If you can tell that your garden spot will be very windy, make a note of that. You'll probably avoid choosing plants that need to be staked.

Extreme heat. A garden on the west side of a light-colored wall will be subject to extreme changes in temperature. In the growing season, when the sun finally reaches this garden, the environment will quickly change from cool shade to hot sun. The wall will reflect heat and light so air temperatures can become blistering. In the winter, there may be problems with heaving of plants as the soil thaws, then freezes again after every warm, sunny day.

Frost. A garden at the bottom of a significant slope may face more frost damage than in uphill areas, because cold air drains down the slope.

Sports equipment. Some plants can tolerate repeated pummeling with your kids' basketballs or Frisbees, some can't. You'll search out the ones that will survive, and recognize that even these survivors won't necessarily look beautiful while they recover from each attack.

Heavy traffic. Human or animal traffic is not to be denied. It's a good policy to work with nature, not against it! Here are two examples:

1. Dogs like to patrol their borders and will often pack down a path along the fence. Gardeners like to garden along their borders. Rather than trying to eliminate the path, leave it undisturbed and plant the garden farther inside the yard. The dogs can still run and the garden will serve an additional function as a screen.

2. Children like to go from here to there. If children have established a path through an area you intend to garden, maintain that path or design an obvious alternate route that is as direct as possible.

Finally! Done with the Site

When you've finished assessing the potential site(s), you can shed the plant's point of view and move back to your designer's stool. From among the likely spots, pick a definite spot for the garden. To narrow the field, read through your list of reasons for the garden, check your budget, and use your notes about the site. Pick the spot that can fulfill the greatest number of reasons for the garden without blowing the budget or putting you into an impossible gardening situation.

At this point, your checklist and/or notes are a complete record of what you've learned in Steps 1 through 4. The time's come to assemble the final ingredients for your design recipe.

LANDSCAPER'S NOTEBOOK

Assessing the Site — Exposure. Your landscape plantings and gardens are exposed to a variety of hazards, from wind and heat, to frost and human and animal abuse. Assess what challenges your site faces and note them in the "Exposure" part of the Site Assessment Sheet.

SITE ASSESSMENT SHEET

The view
- area is seen mainly from:_____

dominating existing features	color	shape	texture	effect

- background could be:_____
- strong lines are:_____
- overall feeling is:_____
- good location for a garden:_____

Sunlight
- hours per day of direct sun: sun (6 hrs or more)   half sun (4–6 hrs)   shade (2–4 hrs)   dense shade (0-2 hrs)
- sunny hours: 8 9 10 11 NOON 1 2 3 4 5 6 7
- seasonal differences in sun at this spot:_____

Soil
- texture: sandy   sandy loam   loam   clay loam   clay   silty loam   silt
- aeration: loose   firm   compacted
- health of existing plants: good   poor   Notes:_____
- depth of existing roots: deep   shallow   Notes:_____

Water availability
- natural water
  - blockers:_____
  - depth of water table:_____
- irrigation via
  - automatic system: spray jets   misters   soakers/bubblers   Notes:_____
  - manual system: Notes:_____
- drainage: very fast   average   poor   standing water   Notes:_____
- runoff from:_____

Root competition
- garden would share root space with:_____
- existing plants that would have to be excluded:_____

Exposure
- natural: wind   extreme heat   frost
- man-made
  - recreational activities:_____   foot traffic:_____
  - pets:_____   other:_____

SAMPLE:

Exposure

- natural: wind   (extreme heat)   frost

 Only near the garage wall where the dryer and furnace exhaust; everything near the house seems pretty protected from wind, etc.

- man-made

  recreational activities:_____   **foot traffic:** _People always ignore walk and cross lawn from drive to porch._

  pets:_____   other: _Low-voltage lighting along front_

  Buried gas line in far north corner

YOUR COPY:

Exposure

- natural: wind   extreme heat   frost
- man-made

  recreational activities:_____   foot traffic:_____

  pets:_____   other:_____

SITE ASSESSMENT SHEET

The view
- area is seen mainly from: _from street, the end of the driveway, and from the front door and living room_

dominating existing features	color	shape	texture	effect
house	tan & cream	boxy	medium	spotted brick, plain, unadorned
evergreen shrubs at house	deep green	clipped round	fine	dark, repetitious blobs
sidewalk to front door	very white	L-shaped	fine	beeline to front door
3 crabapple trees	white flowers	mushroomy	medium	nice, but not really part of house front, too far away
antique water pump	black iron	vertical	coarse	gets lots of attention

- background could be: _the house, the shrubs along the front_
- strong lines are: _the sidewalk, the vertical columns on the porch, the pump upright like a statue_
- overall feeling is: _formal, practical_
- good location for a garden: _Around the pump? Along the front of the house and shrubs? Near trees?_
  But full sun farther away from the house and shade under the crabapples

Sunlight
- hours per day of direct sun: sun (6 hrs or more)   (half sun (4–6 hrs))   shade (2–4 hrs)   dense shade (0-2 hrs)
- sunny hours: (8   9   10   11   NOON)   1   2   3   4   5   6   7
- seasonal differences in sun at this spot: _None by the house; it blocks the sun all year. Shady area near tree. Changes to full sun when there are no leaves._

Soil
- texture: sandy   sandy loam   (loam)   clay loam   clay   silty loam   silt
- aeration: loose   (firm)   compacted
- health of existing plants: (good)   poor   Notes: _Seems OK; shrubs grow fast. Sucklings on crabapples._
- depth of existing roots: (deep)   shallow   Notes: _Lawn is really deep rooted; shrubs may be less so._

Water availability
- natural water
  - blockers: _Always dry right near house because of overhanging roof, garage blocking rain._
  - depth of water table: _Unknown, but former owners said had really deep well._
- irrigation via
  - automatic system: spray jets   (misters)   soakers/bubblers   Notes: _Turn on whenever big lawn jets do._
  - manual system: Notes: _____
- drainage: very fast   (average)   poor   standing water   Notes: _Some areas puddle up for a day after rain._
- runoff from: _Downspouts empty the whole roof at both ends of shrub row._

Root competition
- garden would share root space with: _Nothing, unless it's out by crabapples._
- existing plants that would have to be excluded: _Lots of taller, fast-growing patches in lawn — quack grass_

Exposure
- natural: wind   (extreme heat)   frost
  Only near the garage wall where the dryer and furnace exhaust: everything near the house seems pretty protected from wind, etc.
- man-made
  recreational activities: _____   foot traffic: _cross lawn from drive to porch._
  People always ignore walk and
  pets: _____   other: _Low-voltage lighting along front_
  Buried gas line in far north corner

▲ Your completed checklist will look something like this. It captures all of the essential information you'll need to continue with your landscape design.

Make a Plant List

The fifth step to successful landscaping is to make a list of plants that fit all the considerations you noted in earlier steps. Select plants that will grow on the site. From among those plants, pick an assortment that fits within the budget, will not tax the caretaker's abilities, and will fulfill the goals you established for the garden.

Choosing Your Plants

Where will you get a set of plants to choose from? There are a great many reference books and articles in gardening magazines to help you find suitable plants. Catalogs are also great sources of information, so long as you take descriptions of the plant's beauty, vigor, and persistence with that grain of salt necessary with advertising, for that is what catalogs must be. That is, if a catalog claims that a plant blooms nonstop from April to frost, don't hold it against the plant if it doesn't live up to its hype.

Choose at least two references that describe not only the plants but the growing conditions preferred by each plant. I recommend using two references because there are just too many plants for any one reference to include them all. Some references have charts that help you quickly identify a number of plants that grow in similar conditions. Others have cultural condition symbols to help you quickly locate suitable plants. Find the format(s) that suits you best. Some of my favorite reference books and tips for using such aids are listed for you on page 152.

SELECT PLANTS THAT MATCH YOUR GOALS

You are interested first and foremost in plants that will thrive on your site. In choosing to match the site first, it may seem that you are focusing only on making the plants happy. That's not the case at all. You haven't lost sight of the fact that this garden is meant primarily to fulfill a person's goals. What you are doing is assembling a realistic set of plant choices from which to meet the main goals.

For example, take a garden with a goal of supplying fragrance to the yard. Suppose that the site is in the shade, with reasonably good soil and ample water. If you concentrate on fragrance first, you

Which plants suit your site? List them here:

*Which plants
match your goals?
List them here:*

_____

_____

_____

_____

_____

_____

_____

_____

_____

_____

_____

_____

_____

_____

_____

_____

_____

_____

_____

_____

_____

_____

_____

_____

_____

may spend some time researching the classic fragrant flower, roses. In looking at pictures and reading about all the wonderful attributes of roses, you may fall in love with them. But it's just wasted time, because when you look into cultural conditions for roses, you'll be told to grow them in full sun. In the shade, roses are sickly, with few, if any, flowers, and the fragrance may be much reduced. If you had started by identifying some plants that grow in the shade, further research would reveal those that are fragrant. Using this method you could have quickly found the fragrant hosta *(Hosta plantaginea)* or blue bush clematis *(Clematis heracleifolia davidiana),* rather than spending your time mourning over a lost rose.

EVALUATE YOUR REFERENCES

In your first look for plants, disregard the pretty pictures and Madison Avenue write-ups on each plant in your reference. Skim the cultural information or charts first. Since you're using more than one reference, you'll find that there is some disagreement between authors regarding the growing conditions preferred by various plants. One may say that a particular plant is equally happy in sun or half sun, another is adamant that the same plant must have half sun. This is common and bound to be a fact of life as long as there are different gardeners with different opinions. Treat these discrepancies as opportunities, just as the child does who gets a different answer from each parent. When authorities of equal stature open this door, take whichever advice you find more credible, or more pleasing!

Don't count on any one reference to tell you everything about a plant. In the cultural information section of your reference books, you will almost certainly read about the plant's sunlight and moisture requirements. Often, but not always, you will learn something about the kind of soil the plant prefers to grow in. There is no way to predict whether you will find comments about secondary site considerations, such as root competition from other plants and exposure.

Don't Play Favorites with Existing Plants

You may already have some plants on hand, if your intent is to rearrange an existing garden. It's best to avoid getting locked into those plants; instead, treat them as if they are just entries in a plant encyclopedia. Put them on the list you make in this step only if they pass muster according to your site assessment and reasons for the garden.

DESIGN BASICS

Right Plant, Right Place

As you do your research, consider only those plants that match your primary site criteria: suitable sunlight, soil, and water. If the plant doesn't seem to be suited to your sun, soil, or water conditions, read no further about that plant. Certainly don't look at its picture! The last thing you need to be doing right now is falling in love with plants that aren't suited to your site, so don't tempt yourself.

Determining What Plants Need

Sunlight is so important to plant success that rarely does a reference fail to specify "sun" or "shade" requirements. If there is some disagreement between the experts when it comes to the amount of light a plant should have, you're probably safe to take the advice that suits you.

Water is also mentioned in most references, but the terms used may be as vague as "dry," "average," and "moist."

Preferred soil texture is often but not always mentioned in plant references. This omission is common proba-

bly because plants typically have more tolerance for a variety of soil textures than they do for various sunlight and moisture conditions.

Look It Up

Do as much research as you can to familiarize yourself with all the plants that are suitable for your site. I consider plant books and encyclopedias to be as important as the plants themselves, because the books lead me in the right direction. See "Recommended Reading" on page 152 for a list of my favorite plant books.

TAKE A CLOSER LOOK

Be prepared to take notes and compare references when doing your plant research.

Evaluating References. Whenever possible, use references, like the one below, that indicate a plant's preference for sun, soil, and water.

Comparing garden entries. There will always be some disagreement between authorities as to best growing conditions. Below, two authors disagree about sunlight required by *Geranium grandiflorum*.

False Alum Root
Tellima grandiflora

Hardy perennial for half sun to sun. Flowers spring into early summer, pale green turning pink. 18–24". Handsome, scalloped leaves form clumps that are nearly evergreen, smother weeds nicely. Purple-leaf variety is available. Slugs can be a problem. Prefers moist soil and some shade but is tolerant of dry soils and sun. Can be grown in clay soils.

Cranesbill
Geranium grandiflorum

Light: Sun
Water: moderate
Bloom: summer

A lilac-flowered geranium, blooms a long time. Thrives in almost any garden soil.

Hardy geranium
Geranium grandiflorum

Blue flowers, blooms late spring to early summer. 1–2 feet in height. Grow in sun or half sun. Hardy in Zones 10–5.

MONITOR SUN EXPOSURE

Never push a plant farther into the sun or shade than the majority of your references recommend if the success of your garden depends on that plant's performance. I have seen plants stop flowering with an hour less sun than their neighboring brothers and sisters, become sick with a half hour less than that, and die within a few weeks when they're 2 hours deeper into the shade. The reverse is also true: Shade plants suffer the same fate when planted in the sun.

WATER WITH CARE

An average amount of water for a garden is 1 inch of water per week during the growing season. That means a wide-mouth container or rain gauge in that spot would fill to a 1-inch depth each week. Sandy soils, which warm up, let water slip by, and dry out more quickly, may require more than 1 inch of water each week to be called "average" in soil moisture. Clay soils may require less than 1 inch per week. Probably the truest test for "average" is whether the soil 3 to 4 inches below the surface feels cool and moist (not wet) almost all the time. That soil is getting average moisture for a flower garden. Soils that dry out to a greater depth between waterings are designated as dry; those that are consistently moist close to the surface are considered moist.

IS YOUR SOIL SANDY OR CLAY?

If the soil is well drained and reasonably fertile, you can grow a great number of everyday garden plants. But there are plants without great tolerance for variation in soils. Plants that require deep, sandy soil often rot over the winter in a moist clay soil. Plants for moist clays are pathetic creatures in sand. Be alert for soil texture recommendations and don't take chances with a plant that prefers a very different soil than you have. Soil texture is very difficult, if not impossible, to change to any great degree. There are a number of desirable plants I tried to grow in my own gardens, but I eventually had to give them up for adoption. In the sandy soils that dominate my own gardens, I cannot make a ligularia, rodgersia, or foxglove truly happy. Those plants now reside in friends' gardens. I have visiting rights. The plants and I are both as happy as possible.

Soggy versus Well Drained

Plant references often recommend "moist, well-drained soil." This does not mean that plant likes soggy soil, the kind that calls for rubber boots. A moist, well-drained soil is soil that has both water and air in it. Imagine a dry sponge, dropped into a tub full of water and left until saturated. When you pick that sponge up out of the water, it's moist but well drained. How so? You saw that the excess water drained out (of the air spaces) as you lifted the sponge, yet if you squeeze it, you see there is more water available. As for plants that like soggy soils, your references will probably describe them as suited for swamps, swales, or marshes.

Preferred soil type is not always described in plant references, possibly because so many plants are tolerant of a wide range of soils. Soil-type entries, such as these, alert the gardener to the exceptional plants.

Dahlia hybrids
Garden Dahlia

Flower: a variety of colors and forms, from 2–3" across to more than 6"

Habit: 1–5', round or erect depending on the cultivar

Blooms: midsumemr to frost

Culture: Sun or part shade, likes moist, well-drained soil

Recommended varieties: There are so many that it is difficult to make specific recommendations. Here are a few favorites: Pink

---

Hibiscus moscheutos
Hardy Hibiscus

Flower: large, saucerlike blooms on sturdy stems; red, pink, or white

Habit: upright to mounded, 3–5'

Blooms: late summer

Culture: sunny, constantly moist areas. Prefers rich soils. Known to grow well in clay where drainage is good.

Monarda punctata
Horsemint, Spotted Bee Balm

Flower: whorls of purple-spotted yellow flowers ringed with showy pink bracts

Habit: upright, leafy stems, 1.5–2.5'

Blooms: summer

Culture: sun or lightly shaded areas, short-lived where summers are very hot. Prefers moist, sandy soil. Mildew can be a problem in dry soils.

Nepeta sibirica
Catmint

Flower: upright stems of deep blue flowers

Habit: mounds of handsome gray-green foliage, 2–3'

Blooms: summer

Culture: sun, well-drained soils. Intolerant of wet soils. Reliable plant for very hot areas.

Recommended varieties: 'Blue Beauty' is shorter than the

Gaillardia grandiflora
Blanket Flower

Flower: disc; orange, yellow, and red bands

Habit: 12–36"

Blooms: midsummer to frost

Culture: sun, well-drained soil. Tolerant of drought and heat. Does not tolerate clay soils, poor drainage.

Recommended varieties: 'Goblin'; shorter flower stems

THE POWER OF pH

Acidity and alkalinity (pH range) of soil is mentioned more often in plant references than soil texture, a fact that I find confuses people and leads to the belief that this measurement is more important than any other when it comes to soil. In fact, this emphasis on pH is a disservice to beginning gardeners. Gardeners have even less control over pH than they do over soil texture.

"Must have acid soil" is the most common pH-related notation you'll find in books. If you see that plant references consistently call for acid soil for a plant, don't try it or depend on it to succeed if you are not sure of your soil pH. You will still find a large number of plants that are not choosy about soil pH from which to select; for these there will be no notation about soil pH.

The pH scale. To explain this point as briefly as possible, soil pH is written as a number, such as 7.0. The pH scale operates like the Richter scale for earthquakes: Each decimal point represents a far greater change from its neighboring number than you imagine. On that scale, 7 is neutral, numbers lower than 7 are acid, and numbers higher than 7 are alkaline, or base.

You may be able to lower your soil pH (acidify it) by one or two decimal points over a period of years by adding organic matter and raising beds above the rest of your garden. You can change it a few decimal points toward base by adding lime every year. Yet most plants grow well in a range of 10 or 15 decimal points, from 5.5 to 6.5 or 7, and above.

When the time comes that you must try to grow acid-loving, lime-hating plants or lime lovers, have your soil tested, check with your county Extension Service for the soil survey of your area, or take a look at native plants in your immediate area. The soil test can tell you the pH of specific soil. The soil survey will give you a good idea of the range of natural pH levels in your area. The look at native plants will give you an indication of soil pH: If rhododendrons and trailing arbutus grow wild in your neighboring woods or blueberries grow in the nearby moist meadow, you may have acid soil. If baby's breath and sweet clover dominate the meadows, you may have alkaline soil.

The Acid Test

To be "punny," the acid test is to look around and see if a plant you intend to grow can be found in neighborhood gardens and at local nurseries that grow plants in their own fields. If it grows in your local area, you can probably grow it.

Understanding Plant References

How a plant responds to competition from other plants and how it handles exposure to wind, frost, foot traffic, and so on is usually written up in plant references as an exception. Whether or not a plant reference mentions such items may depend on the author's experience. You may read that a plant is very sturdy in the wind — a plus if your site is windy. A statement such as "requires staking in windy areas" may cause you to exclude that plant if your site is windy and caretaker time is limited.

More often, there will be no mention of such things as how a plant responds to heavy root competition or whether it performs well in repeated frosts. Don't fret over these omissions. Remember the enchantment of gardening? One of the reasons a garden changes over time is that gardeners replace plants that they have learned more about. Competition from other plants and exposure are secondary site considerations because most plants don't fail outright because of such conditions. They simply don't do as well over time as other plants in the area and so become candidates for change.

Refining the List

Once you're convinced a plant will grow on the site, give a brief thought to whether it will tax your budget or caretaker. No need to drop one plant off the list solely because it may be expensive or require some extra maintenance. However, if you find that all of your selections so far have the potential to be financial or maintenance burdens, start vetoing plants for this reason to avoid vexing the caretaker or blowing the whole budget.

BE KIND TO THE CARETAKER

As for knowing that a plant will be a chore for the caretaker, you may or may not get advice from your references. Look for notations that hint at required maintenance, such as "requires staking," "can be invasive," and "susceptible to powdery mildew." Some references list common insect and disease problems for each plant but make no mention of everyday maintenance. I've often wished for a good garden maintenance book that gets specific about handling particular plants. Until it comes, I will continue to keep my own notes on each plant I've grown. Whenever I learn some new maintenance tip, I write it down on the page in the binder for that plant. In this way, I have built a personal reference that helps me match plants to a caretaker. On page 60) is a chart to help you until you build up your own base of information.

ARE GARDEN GOALS MET?

When you find a plant that will thrive on your site and is no problem in terms of budget or maintenance, it's a finalist for the list you're making. Suited in every other way, it now either fulfills a reason for the garden's existence and goes on the list or doesn't fit this last test and is discarded. Characteristics such as color, fragrance, even suitability for cutting, are commonly listed in references. But for information about plants that attract birds or butterflies, flowers suitable for drying, culinary uses of plants,

---

Keep Expense in Line

How can you tell whether a plant will be expensive? If your reference is a catalog, it's usually easy to compare costs. But in other references, your clue to expense may be comments about growth rate or rarity: "extremely slow to establish," "unusual variety," or "should be used more." If a plant takes a long time to grow, the grower must care for it longer than the average plant and charge more to recoup the extra cost. If it's an unusual variety, fewer growers carry it. Even if an unusual plant is not more expensive, the search to find it may be expensive in terms of your time.

What site conditions may affect your plant choices?

DECIPHERING THE DESCRIPTION

Plant Description	Good Points	Bad Points
Do not allow to dry out Water deeply during dry spells Needs constant moisture Requires plenty of water	May love the area by your downspout.	Don't go on vacation without arranging for regular watering.
Does particularly well in dry soils	Can tolerate drought.	May rot if overwatered.
Cut back late in winter Cut back after flowering Shear in midsummer Pinch early in the season	Can be kept looking good in non-blooming seasons.	Will be lank or ugly at some point if not pruned.
{*} may be a problem (the {*} is a pest or disease such as aphids, slugs, or mildew)	You know what to look out for.	Must be inspected regularly; even when grown in the best conditions, pests may need control.
Deadhead regularly	Blooming time can be extended.	Old flowers have to be removed to prolong the blooming time.
May need staking Some support needed	At least you've been forewarned!	Plant will sprawl on neighbor plants or break off unless given support in spring and kept tied to the support.
Spreads quite freely Invasive Fast ground cover Creeps rapidly	Plant can cover a large area quickly	Plant pops up where not wanted; digging out underground runners or cutting plant back will be a regular task.
Self seeds freely	Free plants!	Seedling weeds
Withstands foot traffic Can grow well in unpromising places	Grows where others won't.	Probably spreads rapidly if not controlled.
Do not overfertilize	Lower fertilizer expense	Care must be taken when fertilizing (lank growth or reduced flowering can result).
Mulch well in colder areas Protect over winter	You'll have a use for evergreen clippings.	Extra fall chores May not be hardy in your zone.
Lift and divide regularly	Free plants!	Extra spring work to keep it neat and vigorous
Slow to establish	Probably a long-lived plant	Neighboring plants will have to be prevented from crowding it for several years: bare space!
Shelter from early morning frost Protect flower buds from frost	If you heed the advice, it can be sited on west side and uphill.	Flowers may be ruined in a frost.

and so on, you may need to use specialty gardening books. The choice of specialty garden books is wondrous, ranging from those that list antique plants for restoring old gardens, to descriptions and uses of medicinal herbs, to recommended larval food and nectar sources for butterflies. Most of the plants found in specialty books are also listed in more general plant encyclopedias, but in the general reference all their possible uses may not be described.

HONE YOUR LIST

There are plants to suit every set of conditions. Find them and put them on your plant list for this garden. Use the common name or botanical name of the plant, whichever is most comfortable for you. However, if you are using a number of reference books, it's a good idea to write down the botanical name or to note which book the plant came from. That's because there are so many different common names for plants that your references may each list the plant under a

BE A PLANT DETECTIVE

Plant Characteristics	What You Need to Know
Flower size, shape, color, and fragrance	Look for a picture of the whole plant: Some beautiful flowers are hidden under leaves. Catalog photos are often enhanced; avoid depending on a specific hue until you see it in a garden.
Season of bloom	Take catalog claims about long-season perennials with a grain of salt
Hardiness	Refers only to ability to withstand cold, not other problems (see Durability, vigor).
Use as a cut flower	Grow enough so the garden still looks full after gathering bouquets.
Use as a dried flower	Select varieties that are pest and diseases resistant.
Ground-covering ability	"Ground cover" does not mean "short"; check height.
Durability, vigor	Overall health, stamina; vigorous plants are usually able to keep growing even under adverse conditions.
Speed of growth • slow, refined, compact • fast, carpets the ground	Usually applied to perennials: judge from second season. Slow growers often live longer and are less work. Rapid spreaders are good for a uniform cover on an area, but they can undermine the varied-but-manicured look.
Experience required to grow (easy to grow, a challenge, and so on)	No plant is easy to grow if it's not in the right place
Response to adverse conditions • tolerates heat • tolerates pollution • tolerates drought	"Tolerates" does not mean "prefers." Refers to natural heat, reflected heat off buildings; does not include heat from dryer and furnace vents, though drought tolerant; needs water to get established.

Hone your plant list.
Note "keepers" here:

_____
_____
_____
_____
_____
_____
_____
_____
_____
_____
_____
_____
_____
_____
_____
_____
_____
_____
_____
_____
_____
_____
_____
_____
_____
_____
_____
_____
_____
_____
_____
_____

READING BETWEEN THE LINES

What the Catalog Says	What the Catalog May Mean
Repeat bloomer	May need faded blooms cut off before the plant blooms again
Good plant for beginner	Vigorous or invasive; gratifying for a while, then annoying
Meadow area, naturalizing plant; good for covering large areas	Spreads by seed and runners; invasive in small areas
Something different (rare, unusual)	Good for impressing other gardeners; expensive
Cover for banks and slopes	Once established, good erosion control
Alternative to lawn	Solid, even cover, often without mowing, but generally won't take regular foot traffic as well as lawn grass does
Ground cover under trees	Usually best when grown under deciduous trees where light and moisture are available in winter
Good for seashore conditions	Tolerates salt spray from roads; usually needs moist air; does not always mean will grow in sand dunes
Persistent pods (stalks, bracts), evergreen or semi evergreen, early color, late color	Extended season of interest, even into winter; check for dormant period: early bloomer that dies back after flowering; late bloomer slow to start growth in spring.
Attracts birds	Birds like to eat seeds or insects on plant; flowers should not be removed or insecticides sprayed.
Brings butterflies	Probably also attractive to hummingbirds for nectar
Attracts bees	Likely to attract butterflies
Flowers shaped like . . . (good likeness of an animal, body part, and so on)	Children love flowers shaped like hearts, turtle heads, birds, etc.
Colorful name (animal related, very descriptive, and so on)	Children like names that tell a story or link a plant to an animal or person.

different common name or call two different plants by the same common name. What one book calls a coneflower, another may call a black-eyed Susan. A third may list both coneflower and black-eyed Susan but assign those names to two completely different plants. Botanical names are more reliable.

Finalizing the Plant List

The list you are compiling is going to serve as a quick reference for you as you design, so also record these vital statistics for each plant: why you selected it, its height, and the flower color. For example, you might record: "Purple coneflower, cut flowers and birds, 3', pinkish." If you selected the plant not for its flower color but for its leaf color, record that instead: "Coleus, cut foliage, 18", maroon or pink leaves."

Now leave room for a little more information on the list, and we'll come back to it later.

Don't Leave Out the Leaves

While we're here, if you've never thought much about leaf color, now is the time. There are many striking foliage colors that can add as much or more to the garden as flower color. All greens were not created equal. From the lustrous dark green leaves of the gas plant (*Dictamnus albus*) to the frilly maroon of perilla (*Perilla frutescens 'Crispa'*) to the downy gray of the artemisias, there is every imaginable foliage color. Look for a description of each plant's foliage in your references. Blue-green, yellow-green, green with white edges, or pink, all are valuable. The leaf color can be pleasing all by itself, and it can be a background color or foil for neighboring plants.

purple coneflower, cut flowers, birds, 3', pinkish

black-eyed Susan, cut flowers, birds, 2', gold

baby's breath, cut flowers, 3', white or pink

gayfeather, cut flowers, 2–3', white

sweet rocket, cut flowers, birds, 3' purple

'fire king' yarrow, cut flowers, 18", red

Ornamental rhubarb, 4', big pretty leaves

Cornflowers, cut flowers, 2–3', blue

Shirley poppy, cut flowers, 18", pastels

Cosmos, cut flowers, birds, 3–4', pink and white

◄ When you find a plant that suits your site and the purposes for the garden, make a note of it. Include on this list the plants' vital statistics, for quick reference.

A Complex Situation

At this point the issue of complexity raises its head. A complex garden is one that will be successful only when a great number of goals are met. If you must select plants that will not only thrive on the site but fit eight other criteria, you will search a lot longer to make a plant list than otherwise. Every plant you select must pass many more tests than a plant for a garden with fewer reasons for being.

Imagine designing a garden that is required to be beautiful, easy to maintain, provide cut flowers, attract hummingbirds and butterflies, have dried flowers and herbs in it, and have fragrant flowers. Think about how you would feel after finding a plant that will grow on your site, seems to be simple enough for a beginning gardener to maintain, is inexpensive, and makes a good cut flower. Not only that but your excitement mounts as you learn that it is also a favorite nectar source for hummingbirds and butterflies. You put it on the list. Now go back to the hunt and find another multiple-purpose plant, and another. Eventually you may start passing over plants that have good cut flowers unless they also provide fragrance or can be dried, because these other garden requirements have not been fulfilled on your list. Sometimes, in designing a complex garden like this, the designer spends more time looking for plants than in any other step of the process, but it is time well spent.

WHEN DO I HAVE ENOUGH?

About 10 plants is a good start. Whether it's a large or small garden, it could be finished with just 10 species. It can also include more than 10 plants, but work with 10 or so at a time as you design. Come back to this step to select more plants after you've gone through the next few steps with your first 10. Too many plants at once can be overwhelming.

Two questions often arise at this point: "Should I use annuals or perennials in the garden?" and "What about color — shouldn't I be looking for specific color flowers?"

ANNUALS OR PERENNIALS?

Although my first love and area of greatest expertise is perennials, I commonly use a combination of perennials and annuals in my designs. In some places, to meet the goals of a particular garden, annuals and perennials are interchangeable. For instance, to design a cut flower garden you could use annuals or perennials or both, since there are both annual and perennial cutting flowers. The same goes for herb gardens, since there are both annual and perennial cooking herbs. In other places, the garden's goals may require use of a certain percentage of annuals or perennials.

ANNUALS VERSUS PERENNIALS

Annuals	Perennials
Can't be expected to survive a local winter in most locations in North America	Live for at least three years
	Usually have a much shorter season of bloom than an annual
Generally have a very long bloom season	Bloom season may be much earlier or later than most annuals
Cost less than a perennial of equal size	Generally cost more than an annual of equal size
Available as "starts" from local garden centers or as seed	Available from local garden centers
	Available by mail in seed or plant form

Look at the goals for your garden and the differences between annuals and perennials to judge whether you should stick to one group or the other.

SOME IDEAS ABOUT COLOR

Unless you have a reason to use a certain color or set of colors, don't worry too much about color now. As you actually place plants in the garden, you'll put pleasing colors together. If the plants on your plant list don't offer any pleasing color combinations, you'll come back to this step and look for more plants. Trust yourself.

Most of the people who ask me about use of color are already aware of what colors look good together. They are dressed in harmonious clothing of their own choosing. This is what they are really asking me: "Is there a special method of manipulating color in a garden?" This is my answer: "The same guidelines you use to dress yourself can serve you in the garden." Once you get beyond the need for this advice, there are many advanced tricks to combining colors. Whole books have been written without being able to cover them all. Really sophisticated use of color is something you should get into after you become proficient in basic design principles.

You should be looking for particular colors in the flowers you select if you have a goal for the garden that specifies a color or color scheme. Maybe the garden is to dress up the patio area, and the patio furnishings all have the same two-color pattern. It's sensible to pick up those colors in the garden and advisable to exclude from your plant list flowers that would not go well with those colors. For a garden that will be seen only in early morning and evening when the light is dim, reflective whites, yellows, and pastel colors are good to use. Where the garden must draw attention to the front entrance, it can be effective to repeat the trim color from the house; on the other hand, you may want to create a more dramatic effect by using a second, contrasting color. On page 66 you'll find a quick lesson in color theory, just to get you started.

EFFECTIVE COLOR

Warm colors act one way:
- Stand out at a distance
- Give the impression of warmth
- Compel, create urgency

Cool colors act another way:
- Disappear at a distance
- Create a cool feeling
- Calm, soothe

Analagous color schemes:
- Consist of 2, 3, or 4 colors that are neighbors on the color wheel, such as blue-green, blue, blue-violet, violet
- Are peaceful, gentle

Complementary color schemes:
- Star 2 colors that are directly opposite on the color wheel, such as yellow-orange and violet-blue
- Are dramatic, stimulating

Monochromatic color schemes:
- Have only one color plus its own shades and tints; i.e., blue plus blues with various amounts of black or white added
- Are safe and sophisticated (and tough to create in a garden)

Polychromatic color schemes:
- Include colors from all around the color wheel (all colors go together in a garden: Green foliage is a great harmonizer!)
- Lend a carnival atmosphere and create the most combinations

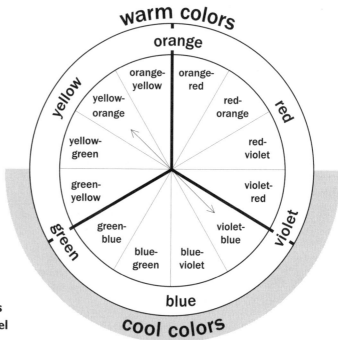

Get out your colored pencils and fill in the this color wheel for easy reference.

What kind of mood are you after?

_____

_____

_____

_____

_____

What colors match your goals?

_____

_____

_____

_____

_____

CONSIDER SHAPE AND TEXTURE

For each plant on your list, draw a symbol that tells you its shape and texture at a glance. This requires another spate of research, learning about the leaves and the habit of the plant. It also may send you back to the books for additional plants, if your first choices do not offer much diversity in shape and texture.

Shape. The shape of the plant is another important design characteristic that may not be spelled out in plant encyclopedias. In plant references, those that mention shape at all may categorize it as "habit." As when you are learning the texture of a plant, you will need to look at plants or pictures of plants to note the overall profile of the plant. Common shapes are round, mat or prostrate, columnar, spire, and vase. Once you start looking for plant shapes, you'll be amazed at how varied they are, and how noticeable different shapes are within a garden composition.

One very good reason to learn the shape of a plant is that it is often your only clue to how many plants you'll need to fill an area.

SHAPE AND TEXTURE: SYMBOLS AND PLANTS

Here are some symbols you might use and combine, along with examples of plants in each category.

PLANT SHAPE	PLANT TEXTURE		
	FINE	MEDIUM	COARSE
Flat, round, mounded • creeping phlox • rockcress • Silver Mound • chrysanthemum • cushion spurge • meadowsweet	• sweet alyssum • baby's breath • moss rose • edging lobelia • dwarf aster • golden marguerite • impatiens • chrysanthemum • candytuft • thyme • sea pink	• petunia • ageratum • bluemist flower • fringed bleeding heart • pearly everlasting • Serbian bellflower • verbena	• peony • lady's mantle • hibiscus • flowering cabbage • hosta • caladium • brunnera • primrose • leopardsbane
Columnar, erect, pillar • bachelor's button • sundrops • false sunflower • daisy • zinnia	• cosmos • kochia • threadleaf coreopsis • purple loosestrife • meadow rue • tall aster • tall marigold	• bee balm • pincushion flower • pot marigold • balloon flower • false indigo • canterbury bells	• pelargonium • comfrey • goatsbeard • sea holly • purple coneflower • bells of Ireland • dahlia
Spike, pyramidal • salvia • cardinal flower • Culver's root • perennial gladiolus • lupine	• liatris • dragonshead • veronica • grape hyacinth • Russian sage • ajuga • liriope	• snapdragon • lupine • jewelweed • gooseneck • astilbe • celosia	• foxglove • ligularia • canna • delphinium • verbascum • bergenia
Vase, flaring • spike • blackberry lily • ferns • yarrow	• flax • fountain grass • carnation • China aster	• butterfly weed • daylily • red hot poker • cleome • toad lily	• plume poppy • iris • gladiola • sweet flag • flowering tobacco • yucca

Texture. This refers to the visual pattern made by the parts of the plant. Coarse-textured plants create bold patterns, visible from a distance of 20 feet or more. Imagine a hosta. Each of its large leaves can be seen distinctly even from 20 feet or so. Fine-textured plants appear to be more of a solid mass from a distance than coarse plants. Picture sweet alyssum. Tiny leaves, tiny flowers all blend together when you stand about 20 feet away. What you see is a fairly solid mat. Medium-textured plants are somewhere in between, like a daylily whose grassy leaves can be discerned at the top and sides of the clump but blend together in the center of the clump.

Rarely do plant encyclopedias list texture in the description of a plant. The designer has to see the plant, see a picture of a plant, or read between the lines to learn about the texture of the plant. It's at this point that designers become frus-trated with standard catalog and encyclo-pedia pictures, which make so much of the flower but rarely show the entire plant. Turn to garden magazines and illustrated garden design books. In these you'll find some excellent photos, although it may take some searching. But what designer minds perusing garden photos?

If you decide you'd rather see the whole plant, head for a garden rather than a garden center, unless the garden center has a good display garden. The standard sale-size plant at the nursery is not usually a good indicator of the mature plant's texture: A daylily with only four leaves is much coarser than the plant will be when it has reached maturity.

Use hosta and sweet alyssum as your benchmarks when you see a plant or a picture of a plant. If its leaves and flowers form a distinct pattern from a distance as hosta does, call it coarse. If it forms a solid mass like alyssum, call it fine.

Armchair Texture Expert

If you cannot go see a plant, here are some clues to help you read between the lines.

- Large leaves usually mean the plant will have a coarse texture: Castor bean plant (*Ricinius communis*), plume poppy (*Macleaya cordata*), and ornamental rhubarb (*Rheum palmatum*) are good examples.
- Lacy, feathery, divided leaves usually lend themselves to fine texture: Many ferns, meadowsweet (*Filipendula vulgaris*), and edging lobelia (*Lobelia erinus*).
- Leaves with variegated edges are coarser than the same leaves of a solid color. This is because the leaf margin is outlined and stands out at a distance. Thus, 'Old Lace' coleus with highly contrasting leaf edge is coarser than 'Molten Lava' coleus with a more uniformly colored leaf; white-edged *Hosta undulata* 'Albo-marginata' is coarser than its all-green parent.
- Highly reflective leaves also contribute to texture because sharp con-trasts are created between the areas of light and shadow. Thus, myrtle (*Vinca minor*), a fairly fine-textured plant, is nonetheless coarser than lawn grass because of its polished leaves.

*Note the shapes and
textures of the plants
you've chosen:*

_____

_____

_____

_____

_____

_____

_____

_____

_____

_____

_____

_____

_____

_____

_____

_____

_____

_____

_____

_____

_____

_____

Putting It
All Together

As of now you've assessed your garden site and selected a specific place or several places for your gardens. You've made sketches of the sites and you've researched and identified the specific plants you'd like to grow. Guess what? You're almost at the halfway point in this 12-step landscape design process. Now comes the finessing — choosing a focal point and really honing in on the garden design. So congratulate yourself on getting this far and let's move on.

Hosta   Alyssum

▲ A plant's texture can best be judged when seeing the whole plant. Hosta, on the left, is coarser in texture than alyssum, right.

step **6** Choose a Focal Point

The sixth step to successful landscape design is to take a closer look at your garden site and pick a point within the garden where you'd like to create extra interest.

This focal point within your garden will always get some extra press, simply because of the design process you're going to follow. So place this point for good effect.

- It can draw the eye into the center of a large garden.
- It can provide visual balance, becoming the third point in a triangle where the viewer and some other important element of the scene are the first and second points.
- It can cause the viewer to align himself or herself with an attractive feature on the horizon.

Taking a Stand

There are no hard and fast rules for selecting a focal point, except this one: To use this design process, you must pick a spot to start! For those who do not have an immovable object already

established as a focal point, this chapter gives some examples to help you make that choice.

In the examples in this chapter, "center," "front," and other directions mean center, front, and so on as seen by the main viewer. Someone at your main viewpoint should feel like he or she is sitting front row center at the theater. If the garden will be seen from more than one point, place the focal point for the primary viewer and then imagine how it will appear to the others. If you adjust the focal point location for a secondary viewer, be sure to come mentally back around to the main viewpoint and check that all is still well from that angle.

THE SHAPE IS STILL TO COME

You may feel the urge to establish a shape for the overall garden. Hold off on this if you can. Imagine the scene from the main viewpoint as an essentially blank canvas, with yourself as a painter. You're deciding now where to put the most attractive part of the painting. You don't have to visualize the shape of the finished composition yet.

List several possible sites in your garden or landscape that can act as focal points:

_____

_____

_____

_____

_____

_____

_____

_____

_____

_____

_____

_____

_____

_____

_____

_____

_____

_____

In some cases, in fact, locking a certain shape into your mind can put constraints on the whole process of painting. Once the painting is finished, you can cut the canvas and get a frame in any shape.

There are certainly situations when establishing a shape for the garden may be unavoidable or perfectly sensible at this point. It's unavoidable if the shape of the garden is dictated by some other features in the scene, such as when the garden will occupy the whole area between a paved walkway and a patio. It makes sense to have a specific shape in mind when the garden is meant to reflect some other feature that is a definite shape, such as a round garden to complement a round gazebo. The garden designer may even be forced to work toward a certain shape, because someone with some great influence has said something like, "This will be a rectangular garden, because that's easier for me to till/put an edge around/work around." Actually, it never ceases to amaze me how often this last situation occurs. People in these circumstances tell me, "This is the spot I was given for my garden."

With or without a definite garden shape in mind, you can keep following this process. You'll find more information for working with a predetermined shape later in this book when we get to Steps 10 and 11.

The Garden at Center Stage

If the garden is meant to be an attraction independent of other features in the yard, you can place the focal point to draw the viewer into any part of the garden you choose. This would be appropriate if the garden area is surrounded by a lawn and it is going to be the "picture" seen out a family room picture window or from a favorite sitting spot in the house. It would also fit for an island garden in the yard near the street

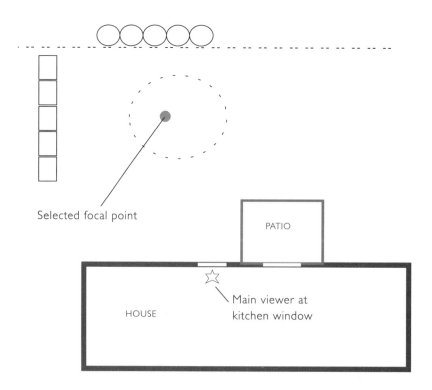

Selected focal point

PATIO

HOUSE

Main viewer at kitchen window

▶ This garden will be out in the lawn. The focal point of this garden does not have any relationship to structures or plants outside the garden itself and could be anywhere within the garden.

end of a driveway, since this garden is serving as a large, detached welcome sign to greet not only guests, but the returning owners.

As you select the focal point for a freestanding garden, you may be setting the tone of the garden toward formal or informal. Placing the focal point in the precise center of an area tends to create a formal look. As the center of interest moves away from the center of the scene, the look becomes more informal. We have probably all seen and admired formal gardens at formal homes: mirror image gardens flanking a path, equal numbers of windows and clipped shrubs on either side of the front door, for instance.

Ask yourself whether this garden you are creating should have a formal look before you place your focal point at the very center of the site. If the garden is in a front yard and the house has a formal, symmetrical look, a formal garden is fitting. If the garden is in a naturally wooded backyard, with a variety of trees and shrubs dotted about in the background, a more informal look may be advisable.

THE GARDEN SHARES ITS STAGE

In some cases, the garden is meant to balance other elements in the scene. Maybe as you look out your family room window there is one large spruce tree to the far right in your field of vision. The tree is already a focal point; it draws the eye because it is massive, tall, and set off by the lawn all around it. You may choose a focal point to the left center of the scene to make the entire view more interesting, rather than building on the existing focal point so far to one side. In doing this, you can create a very pleasant effect by thinking

The Garden as a Side Dish

If your garden is meant to dress up some existing feature, such as a piece of statuary, a bench, an ornamental tree, or the front door, your focal point is that existing feature. Unless that existing feature can be moved, the focal point is already selected; you can jump right to Step 7 and then Step 9 in designing your garden.

of your viewer, the existing focal point, and your new focal point as three corners of a triangle.

Taking Aim: Pointing to Another Feature

When there is something attractive in the background, the focal point of a garden in the foreground can draw the spotlight to that feature on the horizon. If the focal point and that attractive background object line up, both will get attention. So an island garden in the front lawn can draw the viewer's gaze to the front door beyond. On the negative side, this effect can cause unattractive background features to become more noticeable. Be sure that when you establish your focal point it doesn't sit on a direct line between the main viewer and the unattractive feature.

There must be something about picking a place to start that goes against gardeners' genes, because locating the focal point is the hardest concept for students to get past. So, gather up your courage or discard your biases, and pick that place to start. There really aren't very many wrong places that you might choose. Trust me, it's all easy sailing from here.

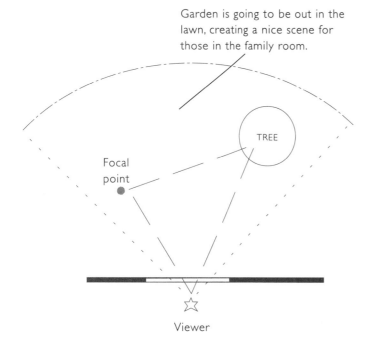

Garden is going to be out in the lawn, creating a nice scene for those in the family room.

TREE

Focal point

Viewer

◄ The focal point could be placed at the far left of the viewer's field of vision to balance the tree to the right. Tree, garden focal point, and viewer are three points of an informal triangle.

The same garden shown above can be given a more formal look by moving the focal point.

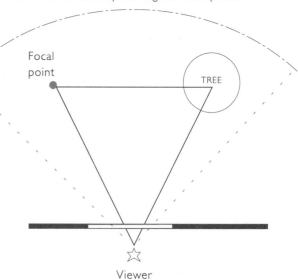

Focal point

TREE

Viewer

▶ The focal point is placed at the same distance from the main viewer as the tree and just as far from the center of the scene as the tree. Tree, focal point, and viewer form an equilateral triangle with a more formal, symmetrical look than in the previous sketch.

*List various view-
points you want to
enhance:*

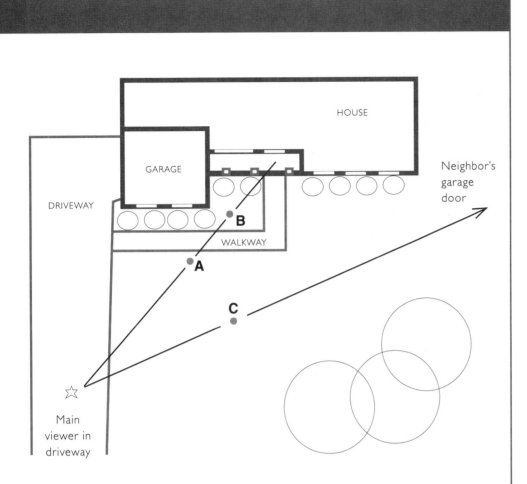

HOUSE

GARAGE

Neighbor's
garage
door

DRIVEWAY

B

WALKWAY

A

C

☆

Main
viewer in
driveway

▲ A and B are better focal points
than C for this viewer, since they
line the viewer up toward the
front door. C, on the other hand,
is in line with the neighbor's
garage door — not the prettiest
view in town!

What garden shapes would work at this site?

_____

_____

_____

_____

_____

_____

_____

_____

_____

_____

_____

_____

_____

_____

_____

Is the garden at center stage or is it sharing space with other features? List the features.

_____

_____

_____

_____

_____

_____

_____

_____

_____

_____

_____

_____

_____

_____

Identify possible focal points.

_____

_____

_____

_____

_____

_____

_____

_____

_____

_____

_____

_____

_____

_____

_____

_____

_____

_____

_____

_____

_____

_____

_____

_____

_____

_____

_____

_____

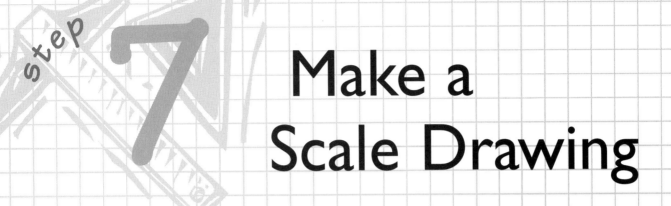

Make a Scale Drawing

The seventh step to successful landscape design is to create a drawing that can quickly tell you sizes of and distances between important objects in and around the garden. In this chapter you'll learn how to show important directions such as north and the number of feet per inch your drawing will represent. You'll measure and draw an existing object within the area that places the garden in reference to fixed objects in the area. And you'll plot the focal point on the drawing and indicate the angle from which the main viewer will be seeing the garden.

Who Needs a Scale Drawing?

A scale drawing allows you to plan exactly where each plant in the garden will go, and how many plants of each type will be needed. But the thought that they must learn to draft a precise, scaled-down version of the garden causes some people to avoid designing altogether. For those people, I say don't give up. You may be able to avoid this step. It may not be necessary for you to draw this particular

garden to scale. If you are willing to work with approximate locations for plant groups and estimated numbers of plants, and if you don't mind continually checking your progress from the main viewing point as you plant, skip this step.

I have done many drawings that were not to scale, and the gardens that came from these drawings have been just as successful as gardens from scale drawings. One person I like very much to work with despises scale drawings, I think. Nonetheless she is building a beautiful garden. The call will come, asking if I can be there next Wednesday because they're ready to do another part of the yard. When I arrive, I am handed a can of spray paint, led to the chosen site and given carte blanche to draw a garden right on the lawn. With two or three different colors, we've worked up some pretty detailed drawings.

But there are times when the designer can't paint the ground today and dig tomorrow. You might have to rely on others for labor, or turn the design over to someone who must estimate accurately the cost of the garden. In these cases it is worth the extra time needed to make an accurate plan that others can follow.

Notes

No Artistic Experience Necessary

Most draftspeople develop their own style of drawing, and some produce intricately penned, ready-to-frame art. Certainly you can aspire to that type of drafting, but it's not necessary for this design process. Remember, this whole process is built on the fact that a garden exists only because a person wants it. The drawing of the garden has to answer that person's needs. As long as the drawing is understandable to that person it is a good drawing.

Let's suppose that Mr. Smith is going to plant his own garden from your design. He needs to know the location of the garden in relation to other objects in the area; specific types, numbers, and sizes of plants needed; and where plants are to be placed. The two drawings below are quite different in appearance and drafting time required, but both would meet Mr. Smith's needs. Each one shows eight

PICTURE IT!

This drawing shows each type of plant with a different graphic symbol. Exact placement of individual plants is shown, and the original drawing was done to a precise scale of 1" = 4'. Compare this to the simpler drawing of the same garden at the right.

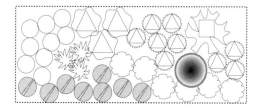

🌼 Queen of the prairie (*Filipendula rubra*), 1 gallon

🌿 Variegated iris (*Iris pallida 'Variegata'*), 1 gallon

◯ Lady's mantle (*Alchemilla mollis*), 4" pot

◒ Ajuga (*Ajuga 'Burgundy Glow'*), 4" pot

△ Salvia (*Slavia splendens*), flats

◯ Periwinkle (*Catharanthus roseus 'Pinkie'*), flats

⬠ Dragonshead (*Physostegia virginiana*), 1 gallon

⬤ Birdbath

This drawing shows each type of plant with a letter code. Quantity of plants is indicated by the number following the letter code, but exact placement of individual plants is not shown. This format requires less drafting than that used to depict this same garden at the left.

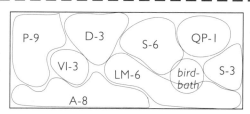

QP - Queen of the prairie (*Filipendula rubra*), 1 gallon

VI - Variegated iris (*Iris pallida 'Variegata'*), 1 gallon

LM - Lady's mantle (*Alchemilla mollis*), 4" pot

A - Ajuga (*Ajuga 'Burgundy Glow'*), 4" pot

S - Salvia (*Salvia splendens*), flats

P - Periwinkle (*Catharanthus roseus 'Pinkie'*), flats

D - Dragonshead (*Physostegia virginiana*), 1 gallon

ajuga plants, for instance: eight individual gray circles with a pie-shaped slash in each represent eight ajuga plants; "A–8" in an irregularly shaped outline also indicates the area to be covered by ajuga plants.

Sharpen Your Pencil

Set yourself up now to do your own drawing. Get a sheet of graph paper, a measuring tape, and a pencil. Letter-sized graph paper with four squares to the inch is easy to obtain and use. A cloth or flexible plastic tape measure in a 50- or 100-foot length is a great tool for garden work. A pencil is recommended over a pen, for a number of reasons. Pencil can be erased, and erasing is almost always required while you're designing. Also, if you design gardens for others, there will inevitably be days when it is colder and wetter than you planned it to be, yet the design must proceed. Pencils write reliably in cold and wet weather.

To illustrate the development of a scale drawing, we'll take as our example a garden to be seen out a family room window, opposing an existing spruce.

YOU SET THE SCALE

First, establish the scale you'll use for the drawing; that is, how many feet of garden each inch on your graph paper will represent. To do this, place yourself at the main viewing point and estimate the overall width of the general garden site.

Divide the width of the area by the number of inches the graph paper has to offer you. Allow for a margin between the drawing and the edge of the paper, which means an 11-inch piece of graph paper with a ½-inch margin at left and right has about 10 inches of drawing space. Compare the answer you get to the number of units in each inch of your paper. If your answer is the same or less than the number of units per inch on your paper, you can make each unit on your paper represent 1 foot. If the answer you get is greater than the number of units per inch on your paper, double or triple the number of units; each unit will represent 2, 3, or more feet. This math exercise helps you avoid a frustrating experience: running off the edge of the paper with a drawing.

Example: Your garden area is about 50 feet wide. Your graph paper has 10 inches of drawing space, with 5 squares per inch.

$$50' \div 10" = 5$$

In this example, 1 square can equal 1 foot (or $1" = 5'$)

Make a note on your graph paper to show that each inch of paper represents a certain number of feet of garden.

Designer's Checklist

Have your tools ready before you head outdoors to do your sketch:

✔ Paper
✔ Pencil
✔ Eraser
✔ Graph paper
✔ Tape measure

DESIGN BASICS

Big Garden, Big Paper?

Using larger paper is a way to show more detail in a larger garden area. I recommend learning to use letter-size paper because it can fit on a clipboard and be taken outside. If you need the detail larger paper gives you, make a sketch that is not to scale but shows the measurements you've made. Then transfer this information to the larger paper while working at a desk or table.

Computer Programs

Computer drawing programs are also great tools for the designer. They can be reproduced and revised endlessly: blown up to show more detail; condensed to show the garden in a larger setting; displayed in sections to show sequence of planting. But the designer who works with a computer drawing program still must know how to set up a scale drawing. My final designs are almost exclusively computer-drawn, but each one starts as a scale drawing on letter-size graph paper or a sketch with measurements indicated.

Which Way "Up"?

Now to orient your drawing, designate which way is "up." Cardinal directions can be helpful. Show north with an "N" and an arrow. It is not necessary that north be at the top of the drawing. This drawing is for the gardener, and the gardener is concerned about what the main viewer will see. For this reason, my drawings are usually oriented so that the main viewer would be at or off the bottom of the paper. The main viewer and the designer are then "looking" at this garden from that particular perspective.

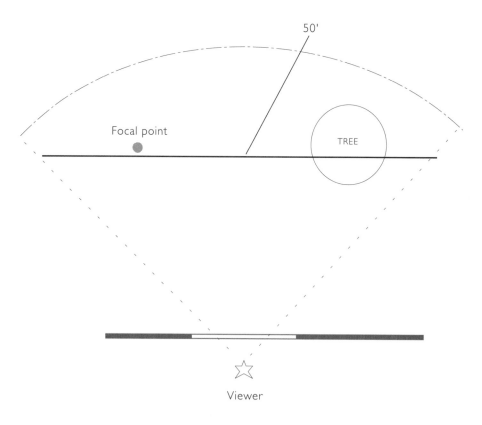

▲ To make a scale drawing, begin by estimating the total width of the garden area. Here, width is 50 feet.

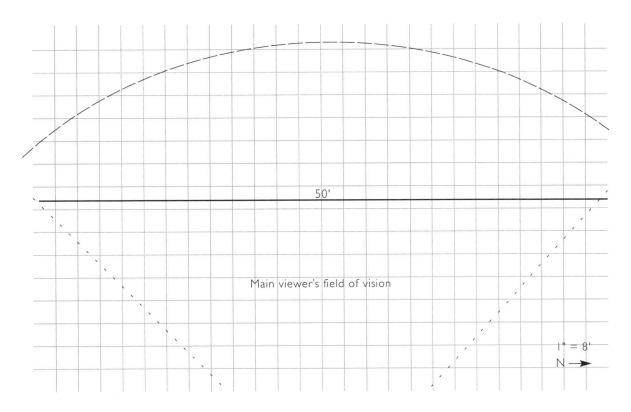

50'

Main viewer's field of vision

1" = 8'

N →

▲ We'll use letter-size graph paper divided into four units per inch. Fifty feet of garden site divided by 10 inches of available paper is 5, greater than our number of units per inch. So we use units per inch times 2 as our scale: 1 inch on the paper represents 8 feet of garden. 50 divided by 8 is 6.25, so a 50-foot line is 6.25 inches long.

SHOW A LANDMARK

To help people reading the design to orient themselves on the site, show one existing, fixed feature. This is a landmark, and will show precisely where the garden will be.

It doesn't matter what the landmark is so long as you can consistently find it and measure from it to other objects in the garden. Square and rectangular objects are easy to represent on graph paper because they can be aligned with the grid lines on the paper. Measurements taken from these objects can be consistently reproduced. Use an object with squared sides as a landmark if you have one. It saves you time because you won't have to square off the drawing. (See the box "Square Off," on page 83.)

Even with an irregularly shaped landmark, squaring off can be skipped if the landmark itself contains a squared-off element. For instance, a kidney-shaped cement patio is not the best landmark, because it would be difficult to know each time you measure whether you're measuring from the same spot. But if right angle lines run through the patio, such as the edges of poured sections, these lines can be your landmark.

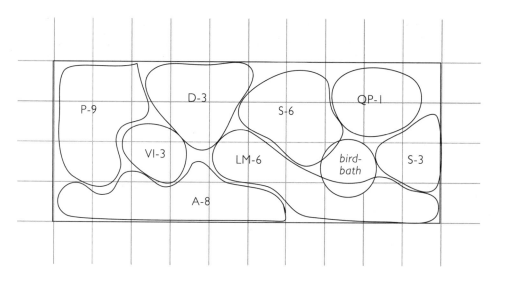

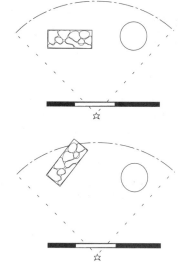

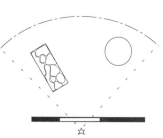

▲ Without a landmark, this garden design could be planted in any of the ways shown at the right. You need to be more specific!

▼ With a square-sided object, such as a patio, in the garden area, you can align your graph paper with the sides of the object. Measurements can be accurately made from its sides, and the garden can be placed relative to that object.

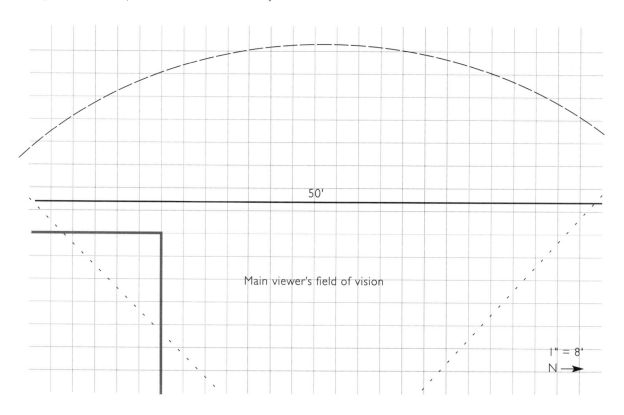

50'

Main viewer's field of vision

1" = 8'

N →

If you do not have a squared-off object to use as a landmark within your garden site, you'll need to take the extra step of squaring off your drawing to a landmark outside the area.

Choose a squared-off object or line toward the main viewer: a wall of the house, a patio, a driveway, or the street. Measure from the landmark within the garden site to the square-sided one outside the site. Take the measurement as close to perpendicular (90°) from the square-sided landmark as possible. Show on your paper what the second landmark is and the distance between landmarks.

Now you can show a specific grid line as parallel to a landmark. Take measurements as necessary from the second, square landmark and locations marked on the drawing in reference to the corresponding grid line.

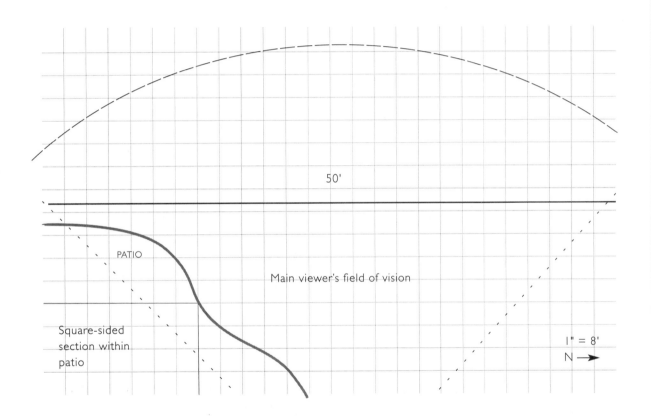

50'

PATIO

Main viewer's field of vision

Square-sided
section within
patio

1" = 8'

N ⟶

▲ Irregular objects such as this curved patio are more difficult to align on the graph paper. Placing the garden in relation to this patio would also be more difficult if there were no specific point that can be placed on the graph paper and located on the patio for measurements. This curving patio contains a poured section with square edges. That square section becomes the landmark.

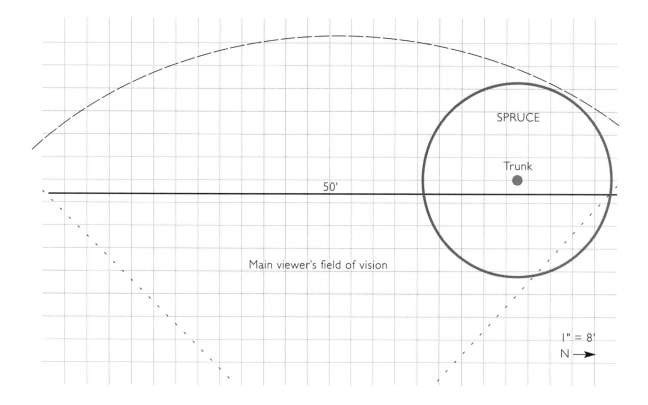

SPRUCE

Trunk

50'

Main viewer's field of vision

1" = 8'

N →

▲ The landmark in our example will be the spruce tree in the garden area. The trunk of the spruce is one point we can use for consistent measurements. We'll also show the spread of its branches. The spruce is on the right-hand edge of the viewer's field of vision, so we draw it far right on the graph paper. The branches of the spruce extend about 8½ feet from the trunk, so the whole tree is about 17 feet across. The spruce is drawn as a circle 2½ inches in diameter (17 divided by 8).

DRAW THE FOCAL POINT

Next, pinpoint the focal point in the actual garden area. Stick a stake in the ground or place a stable, visible object where you believe the focal point should be. Go to the main viewing point and see whether the spot you've marked is where you want the viewer to look. Adjust as necessary. If you have a helper, you can do this without walking back and forth between the focal point and main viewing point.

Place the focal point on the graph paper. Measure from the focal point to the landmark(s) that you have on your paper. Make all measurements parallel to the sides of the square-sided land-mark you drew or indicated on your drawing. You need two measurements:

- Distance to the right or left (per the orientation of your drawing) between focal point and landmark
- Distance above or below the land-mark from the focal point

Find the vertical and horizontal grids on the graph paper that correspond to the distances you measured from the landmark. Mark the spot where these two grid lines intersect as the focal point. Placing the focal point in relation to the landmark as shown in the bottom drawing on the opposite page.

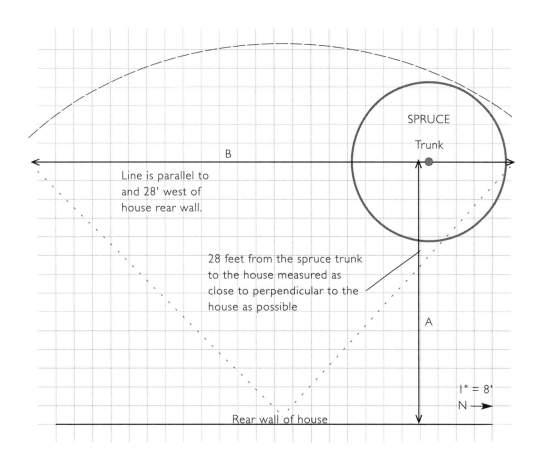

SPRUCE

Trunk

B

Line is parallel to
and 28' west of
house rear wall.

28 feet from the spruce trunk
to the house measured as
close to perpendicular to the
house as possible

A

1" = 8'

N →

Rear wall of house

◄ The spruce is a good
landmark, if it can be
aligned with the grid on
our paper. The nearest
fixed, square-sided object
is the rear wall of the
house. Measure from the
spruce trunk to the house
along a line perpendicular
to the wall (A). Mark a
line on the graph paper
that passes horizontally
through the spruce trunk
to show that it is 28 feet
from and parallel to the
wall (B). Now any point
on the design can be
established by remeasur-
ing to both the spruce
trunk and the wall.

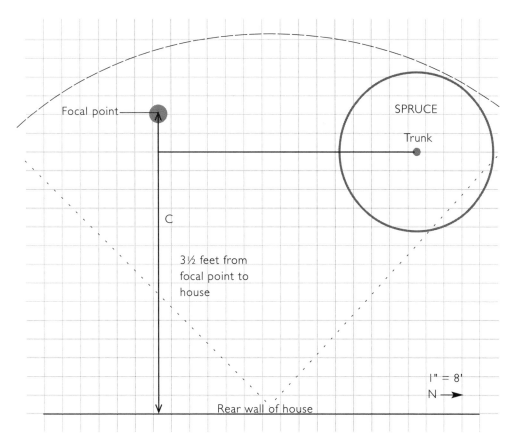

Focal point

SPRUCE

Trunk

C

3½ feet from
focal point to
house

1" = 8'

N →

Rear wall of house

◄ From spruce trunk to
focal point, lay a tape
measure parallel to the
wall of the house — 28
feet (3½ inches) going
to the left of the spruce
trunk. But how far up or
down from the spruce?
Measure from focal point
to the wall of the house,
with tape measure perpen-
dicular to the wall (C). The
focal point is 32 feet (4
inches) from the house —
4 feet (½ inch) farther
from the house than the
spruce tree.

▶ Measuring from a square-sided object within the garden area is simple. Take all measurements from a distinct point on the patio, the corner shown here. Measuring parallel to the north-south axis of the patio, the focal point is 28 feet south of the patio corner. Then measuring parallel to the patio's east-west axis, the focal point is 4 feet west of the patio corner.

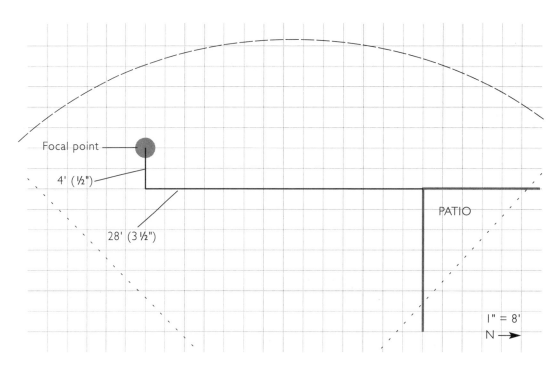

Focal point

4' (½")

28' (3 ½")

PATIO

1" = 8'
N →

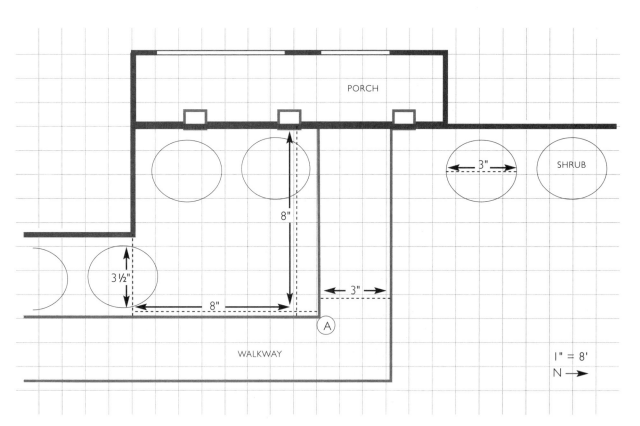

PORCH

3"

SHRUB

8"

3 ½"

8"

3"

A

WALKWAY

1" = 8'
N →

▲ This front door garden is a snap to draw to scale, with so many straight lines and right angles. The first point put on paper was the corner of the walkway (A). Everything else was measured from there.

Don't Forget the Main Viewer

Finally, put an arrow on your paper to show where the garden area is in relation to the main viewer. If there are multiple viewers of equal importance, show these. Secondary viewpoints don't have to be indicated.

Now you have everything you need to draw the whole garden to scale as you design it, one step at a time.

▼ There's no need to clutter up the drawing with the lines showing the main viewer's field of vision. But it is important to show where the main viewer is in relation to the drawing, especially if the viewer is not looking at the garden from center bottom of the page. Arrows in this drawing place the main viewer, as well as the secondary viewpoint, in relation to this garden site.

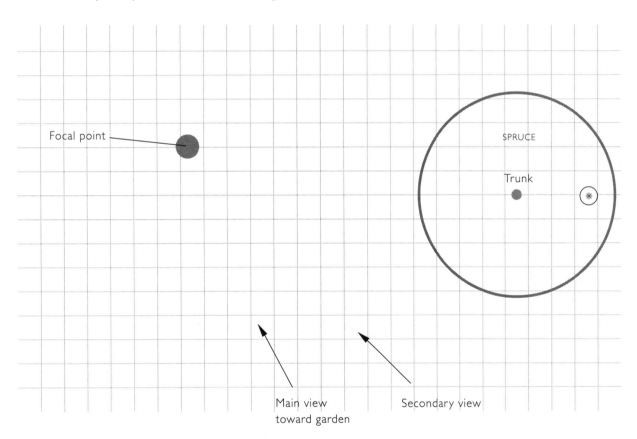

8 Place the Focal Point Plant

The eighth step is to choose a plant from your plant list that has one or more particularly attractive features. Make one or a group of these plants the focal point of your garden.

Any plant can be a focal point plant. Plants that are taller and more brightly colored than their companions are naturals, but even the most common plant can be the center of interest when it is well placed. You've chosen the place and you'll keep the spotlight on that place throughout the rest of the design process.

Making the Best Plant Choice

A focal point plant can have especially attractive flowers, foliage, or texture, or it may be distinctively shaped. A clump of spirelike lupines (*Lupinus* species or hybrid) is spotlighted when placed among mounded golden marguerite (*Anthemis tinctoria*) or sweet william (*Dianthus barbatus*). But notice how a common yellow-green hosta can stand out in a bed full of finer textured, darker green myrtle. A patch of flat, smooth creeping phlox (*Phlox subulata*) surrounded by spikey iris leaves (*Iris germanica* hybrids) and vase-shaped fountain grass (*Pennisetum alopecuroides*) can be a pool for visual meditation.

The plant you choose to fill the focal point may echo some important feature from outside the garden: the shape of the spruces in the background, the texture of the walls of the house, the color of the front door. If you echo such a feature, be sure to keep the focal point plant from getting lost in its larger partner: a red-flowered plant directly in front of a red front door will blend into the door; a coarse-textured hosta may be wasted in front of a coarse-textured fieldstone wall.

ANNUAL AND PERENNIAL LEADERS

Some special notes about focal point plants.

- **Reliability.** A focal point plant should be a reliable plant. Annual plants that suffer heat decline, a midsummer resting phase accompanied by reduced flowering, are not the

List your focal point plant choices:

best candidates for focal points. Pansies, sweet alyssum, and snapdragons are three known to experience heat decline. They can be kept looking neat if the caretaker has time for constant removal of spent flowers, but other annuals such as globe amaranth *(Gomphrena globosa)*, mule marigolds, or impatiens all require less maintenance and will keep blooming strong throughout the growing season.

- **Long-lasting.** Perennial plants that go dormant during the growing season can be embarrassments when given so much uninterrupted attention: Columbine *(Aquilegia canadensis* and its hybrids), old-fashioned bleeding heart *(Dicentra spectabilis)*, and perennial bachelor's button *(Centaurea montana)* can all look exceedingly ragged after bloom. Good perennials for focal points have a long blooming season or have attractive foliage, texture, or shape to carry them through nonflowering periods. Fringed bleeding heart *(Dicentra eximia)* coral bells *(Heuchera* spp.), and the dwarf blanket flowers *(Gaillardia grandiflora* varieties, such as 'Goblin' and 'Baby Cole') have one or more of these features to commend them for center stage.

WORK WITH GROUPINGS

If the focal point is large enough, a group of perennials that contributes successive bloom seasons or works as cover-up for failing companions can substitute for the single focal point species. This requires careful planning to maintain enough interest in the focal point at all times, but when successful, it can be very attractive. One of my favorite combinations of this kind for a sunny focal point is tulips, Asiatic lilies *(Lilium* hybrids), and perennial fountain grass *(Pennisetum alopecuroides)* together. The tulips and lilies provide color in the spring and early summer when the grass is not yet contributing; the grass carries the area in later summer and fall.

For the half shade, I like to use old-fashioned bleeding heart *(Dicentra spectabilis)* with late astilbes *(Astilbe arendsii* hybrids) and Japanese anemones *(Anemone hybrida)*. In the shade, Virginia bluebells *(Mertensia virginica)*, painted fern *(Athyrium Goeringianum pictum)*, and fall cimicifuga *(Cimicifuga simplex)* work well together. Many plant books have charts for selecting groups of plants that will provide continuous bloom.

LEADERS MUST HAVE IMPACT

How many plants should you use in the focal point? One or many, enough to make a visual impact when seen from the main viewpoint. Exactly how many plants are needed hinges on how large a spot the plants will fill and how much space there should be between individual plants.

Warning: If you must know the precise number of plants needed, you are in one of those situations where you must draw your design to scale. If you had hoped to skip Step 7, sorry!

Determine size. How large should the focal point be? I recommend that a focal point plant or group of plants be at least as wide as 5 percent of the distance between the main viewer and the focal point. If the garden is next to a patio and the main viewer will sit 10 feet away, a single 6-inch-wide plant is enough (10 feet × 5 percent = .5 feet or 6 inches). When the garden is 50 feet away, a group of plants 2½ feet wide is needed. The focal point can be wider than this, or a patch of very tall plants can do as well as a wider group of short plants in some cases. You can experiment with this by putting objects of different widths and heights at the focal point and looking at them from the main viewing point. I've used everything from picnic coolers to small children placed at the focal point to check how large an object must be to have impact on the main viewer.

Determine spacing. Once you've determined how large an area you want to fill with a focal point plant, think about how much space each individual plant in that area should have. Figuring how many plants of a specific type it takes to fill a given area is simple if you know the height and shape of the plant. A round plant that is 2 feet tall can obviously spread 2 feet wide. A columnar plant is taller than wide, a prostrate plant wider than tall. Here are some estimates that you can use, if your plant

encyclopedia hasn't specified spacing of plants:

- Round plant: Allow for width same as height.
- Mounded plant: Allow for width 1½ times the height.
- Prostrate plant: Allow for width 4 times the height.
- Columnar plant: Allow for width ½ of height.
- Narrow column or spirelike: Allow for width ⅓ of height.
- Vase-shaped plant: Allow for width same as height.

To save yourself a lot of erasing, until you become accustomed to filling plants of a given size in an area, work with sets of cutout circles of varying sizes. Move the cutouts around until they fill an area as neatly as you please, and then draw.

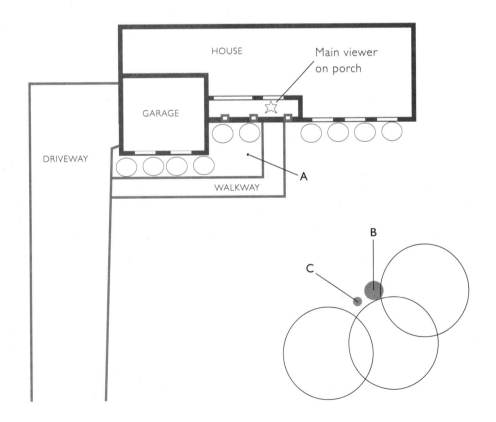

◀ The size of the focal point varies with the distance from and impact on the main viewer:
(A) Focal point in a garden 10 feet from viewer can be a single plant, 6 inches wide (10 feet × 5 percent).
(B) Focal point in a garden 45 feet away is much larger, 28 inches (45 feet × 5 percent).
(C) Plants that are very bright or tall can do justice to a minimum-size focal point. If there are few dramatic differences among plants on your list, plan a larger spot. Here, twice the minimum.

▶ This 4-foot focal point can support 2 to 40 plants, depending on plant size.

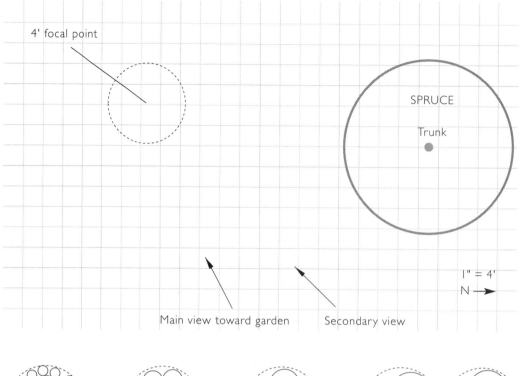

4' focal point

SPRUCE

Trunk

1" = 4'

N →

Main view toward garden　　Secondary view

40 plants 6" wide

11 plants 12" wide

4 plants 18" wide

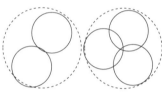

2 or 3 plants 2' wide

PREVENT STICKER SHOCK

Plants can of course be spaced more closely or farther apart than estimated here. This is when a budget is critical, because budget as well as aesthetics can be a reason to adjust plant spacing.

Think about the budget you have. The preceding space estimates are to be used where plants can be allowed to mature before the ground between them disappears. Does this garden have to look full right away? If so, crowd the plants beyond the estimate. Can the gardener wait for the full-to-bursting look? Give the plants more room than the estimate.

Still think about the budget, but now also regard the dollar component.

Look at the focal point you've just filled with plants. The entire garden may well contain 10 to 20 times as many plants, spaced per the estimates above, and look full only at the end of its growing season. Look at the average price of an annual and a perennial at your local nursery. Multiply plants at the focal point spot × 20 × average plant cost. Is there enough money for that many plants? Good, continue at pace. Is there money left over to achieve an instantly full look? Still fine; you can crowd plants if necessary. Is the budget inadequate? Don't despair. There are adjustments the designer can make to save the day.

If the budget can't accommodate the dollar figure from the equation above, numbers of plants can be reduced in other parts of the garden without negatively affecting your time budget. Those opportunities to adjust plant numbers are explained in Steps 9 and 10. Regardless of what your dollar budget says about the rest of the garden, leave the focal point as full as your time budget allows, and forge ahead.

Protecting the Garden's Beauty

What about aesthetics? Is the look of the garden hurt by crowding or wide-spacing plants? There are some strong personal opinions on this issue among gardeners, my own among them. I will try to maintain a detached perspective and explain the pros and cons involved. Be forewarned, the answer depends on (guess what?!) the goals of the garden.

IS CROWDING GOOD OR BAD?

Plants crowded closer than the preceding estimates can be attractive when they are intended to grow into a solid mat. A plant meant to be admired for its shape must have enough room to mature without tangling with neighboring plants. A plant chosen for its shape but crowded for immediate fill must be given room via thinning at the appropriate time. Crowded plants are stressed plants, taxing the water- and nutrient-holding capacity of the soil, impeding air circulation and the ability to grow sturdy stems. Thus, crowding can look good or bad, and it usually increases caretaker time to keep a crowded bed healthy and beautiful.

DESIGN FOR RESULTS

Think about these two planting situations and all the possible design solutions:

Desired	Designed
Quick results Lots of color at the front door Limited budget Knowledgeable caretaker with moderate amount of time to spend	An annual garden, with plants somewhat crowded **or** A primarily perennial garden with a number of annual areas for immediate color. Use of perennials will reduce subsequent years' investment in plants. Perennials used are aggressive, for quick fill, but will need division annually to be kept within their own areas.
Inexpensive, enduring, low-maintenance garden Long season of interest around the patio Quick results are not essential	A varied planting of slow-growing, stay-in-their place kinds of perennials, widely spaced

IS WIDE SPACING GOOD OR BAD?

Plants spaced wider than the estimates take longer to form a continuous mass. Perennial plants spaced more widely than the estimates will fill in eventually, but some perennials gallop, some march, and some poke along toward that end. Annuals spaced wider than the estimates can look sparse, or they can look like individual bouquets, depending on the way spaces between plants are treated. Widely spaced plants put less stress on each other for nutrients, water, and air, but weeds can take root between them. Thus, wide spacing can look good or bad, and it requires more designer time and more control to make a wide-spaced planting look good.

Two's Company — Three's Formal or Informal

If your focal point contains more than one plant, you cannot avoid drawing lines as you set that group of plants in place. Lines lend to the feel of a garden, formal or informal. If you have a large number of plants in the focal point, the group can be shaped to adhere to the feeling you want in the garden. Symmetrical shapes, regular curves, and precise angles tend to feel formal, while asymmetrical shapes, sweeping curves, and wide, unmatched angles are more informal. Common advice to gardeners is to use uneven numbers if you want an informal look, and sometimes even if you want formal. Uneven numbers do have a tendency to fall into informal groupings, but they can be placed formally. Your awareness of the look you want is the key. Note how an even num-

The Plot Thickens

The designer doesn't have to make a blanket statement: to crowd, to plant moderately, or to spacewidely. Plant choices have to be factored in: There are fast growers, slow growers, annuals, and perennials. Arrangement of plants makes a big difference: A good designer can make a pretty garden with very few plants, carefully placed. So there are innumerable choices for the designer who understands both the reasons for the garden and the characteristics of individual plants on the list.

▶ Notice how the same number of plants can create both formal and informal arrangments simply by the way in which they are placed in the landscape.

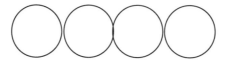

4 plants arranged formally

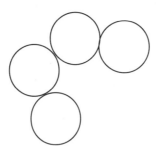

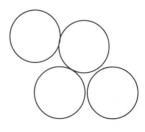

4 plants arranged informally

ber of plants can be arranged both formally and informally. We'll do more with lines in the next step.

Back to the Drawing Board

As you draw your focal point plant on your design, you can use the symbols from your plant list. These can tell you at a glance each plant's important characteristics. Along with shape and texture, the symbols can tell you about plant height and seasonal interest. Plant height is usually indicated with different thickness of line, and winter interest can be indicated by shading in the plant symbol.

Blooming season interest can be shown with colored fills. In a perennial garden, spring-blooming plants may all be green, summer bloomers red, fall bloomers blue.

It's not essential to show all of a plant's characteristics on the design itself. You choose what to show. Make a key that includes any essential information the plant symbols could not show. With a detailed key, you can use simpler outlines to show where a plant or group of plants will be.

Use a key that identifies each species in the design with a unique symbol. That might be a letter, a graphic symbol, or a combination of the two. As you design, you will eventually want to change a plant already drawn into the design. It's simpler to change one species name in a key than to change individually labeled plants.

The illustrations in this book use a number of different symbol and key systems. There is no "best" system. Drawings are to be used by people, and people have different needs, so be flexible.

Finally, you have a plant placed in your design. Now you can start putting plants down in bunches.

▼ It is helpful to show the important plant characteristics somewhere on the drawing. "Important" characteristics vary from garden to garden, depending on the reason the garden is being planted.

| WINTER INTEREST | PLANT HEIGHT | | |
	SHORT	MEDIUM	TALL
Shade the symbol to indicate evergreen leaves, attractive stalks, or pods in winter. Degree of shading can show varying amount of interest.	Lightweight, thin, or gray lines are used for shortest plants.	Line weight increases to show taller plants.	Heaviest or blackest lines indicate tallest plants.

▼ Details of plant height, texture, shape, and winter interest are conveyed via graphic symbols. You may want to make note here of symbols you'd like to use for your plants.

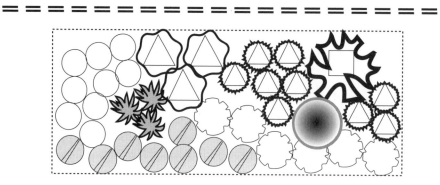

Queen of the prairie (*Filipendula rubra*)

Variegated iris (*Iris pallida variegata*)

Lady's mantle (*Alchemilla mollis*)

Ajuga (*Ajuga 'Burgundy Glow'*)

Salvia (*Salvia splendens*)

Periwinkle (*Catharanthus roseus 'Pinkie'*)

Dragonshead (*Physostegia virginiana*)

Birdbath

Notes

_____

_____

_____

_____

_____

_____

_____

_____

▼ In this example, simple symbols indicate individual plants. Information about blooming season, color, shape, and texture are included in the key. You may want to make note here of the characteristics you want to include in your key.

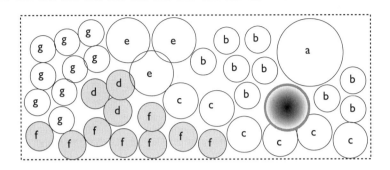

a - Queen of the prairie: 4–5" pink plumes in July, nice seed heads, attractive large leaves

b - Salvia: cream or lavender spike flowers all summer, 18–24"

c - Lady's mantle: mounded, with foamy, yellow-green flowers in May-June; 12"

d - Variegated iris: violet flowers in spring; bold, striped leaves nice all year; 12–18"

e - Dragonshead: 2–3' leafy spikes, pink flowers in July-August

f - Ajuga 'Burgundy Glow': ground hugger, maroon and white on leaves, blue spikes in May, 6"

g - Periwinkle: mounded plant with lustrous, dark green foliage; rose flowers all summer; 15"

══ ══ Privacy fence

·········· Bed edge, 4" deep, flexible plastic root barrier

Birdbath, stone, 30"

Notes

_____

_____

_____

_____

_____

_____

_____

_____

▼ This drawing emphasizes plant use rather than placement or appearance of individual plants. You may want to make note here of the different plant uses you are planning.

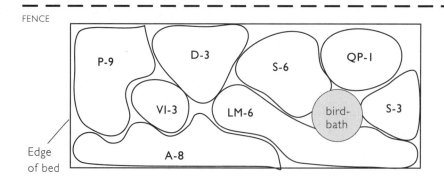

QP - Queen of the prairie *(Filipendula rubra):* perennial cutting flowers, birds

VI - Variegated iris *(Iris pallida 'Variegata'):* perennial cutting flowers, winter interest

LM - Lady's mantle *(Alchemilla mollis):* perennial, cut foliage and flowers

A - Ajuga *(Ajuga 'Burgundy Glow'):* perennial winter interest, hummingbirds

S - Salvia *(Salvia splendens):* annual, hummingbirds, cutting flowers

P - Periwinkle *(Catharanthus roseus* 'Little Pinkie'): annual cutting flowers

D - Dragonshead *(Physostegia virginiana):* perennial, cutting flowers

Notes

9 Frame the Focal Point

The ninth step to successful landscape design is to choose and place groups of plants to highlight the focal point plant. Our minds have some predictable habits. We like to underscore or circle important items. We like to see beautiful vistas brought to crisp focus by a suitable frame. The designer caters to these habits by framing points of special interest in a garden. As seen by the main viewer, the focal point should be framed with harmonious plant groups.

Candidates for a Frame

Select a plant from your list that is different in some significant way from the focal point. The difference may be in height, texture, shape, foliage color, or flower color. Place one or more groups of this second plant so that the main viewer sees the focal point surrounded (but not hidden), underlined, backed, or flanked. The result of this framing will be to maintain interest at the focal point while introducing a second source of beauty to the garden.

FRAMES HAVE SEVERAL PURPOSES

Take care when selecting a really good frame. Picture the best framing job you've ever seen at an art gallery, a friend's house, or in your own home. The frame and matte have two important functions: to set the picture apart from the wall on which it hangs, and to harmonize with the picture by picking up some feeling, color, or texture in the artwork itself. An intricately carved frame can look wonderful against a solid color wall but can be lost against one with heavily patterned wallpaper. A gray matte can do wonders to pick up a singular gray tone in a painting but may be out of place around a sunny pastel.

With the plant choices that come immediately after setting the focal point, you are matting and framing

Focal Points Other Than Plants

If your garden is designed to highlight a nonplant feature of the yard, such as a birdbath, sundial, or fountain, that feature is the focal point and your first plant choices will be the frames.

your center of interest. The framing plants should look good against their background. They should be distinct from the focal point but be pleasing companions at the same time.

You can use one or several different plants to do this framing, to create frames that are formal or informal in feeling, to establish color schemes, and to begin leading the eye around the garden.

ONE-PLANT FRAMES

The simplest frame is to plant the second plant on all sides of the focal point plant. This is the horticultural equivalent of setting an interesting item at the center of a solid-color table or pedestal. From all angles, this one-two combination will be effective.

If your garden doesn't have to appear the same from all angles, you may choose to place the second plant only to the right and left of the focal point, only as an underline, or only as a backdrop. Placing the second plant to the right and left has the same effect as

placing gateposts at the end of a driveway or a pot of flowers on either side of the front door. The flanking objects call attention to whatever lies between them. (This is a fact that many people don't realize, or they wouldn't put matching bushes on either side of their garage doors!)

A plant that will frame by underlining the focal point appears only in the front and is usually shorter than the focal point plant. This technique is attractive. Notice how many people use it to underline their home and foundation plantings with a border of annuals.

A backdrop for the focal point is generally a frame of taller plants, but if the garden slopes up and away from the main viewer, even a short plant can be used as a backdrop.

Envision a good frame and draw its shape on your paper. Sometimes there are items in the garden area that get in the way of the perfect shape for your frame: walkways, walls, and so on. Before you compromise on your ideal, look at ways you can work around such

▶ While you place plants and frame them, pretend that unplantable surfaces aren't there. Draw the frames you want, and plant only where you can. Here, the desired effect is an A group of plants in front of the door, surrounded by a B group. Though the walkway bisects the groups, the mind's eye can fill in gaps and recognize partial shapes!

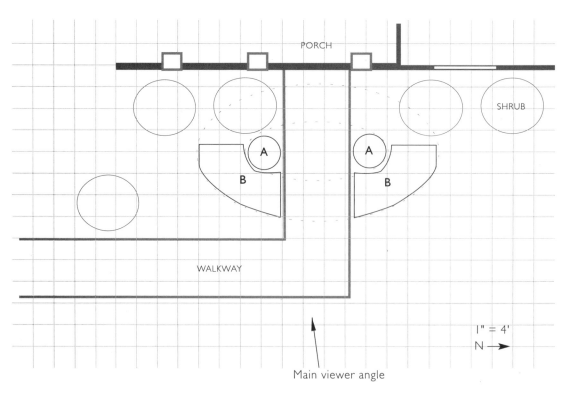

areas. For example, working around a walkway is shown on the opposite page.

COMBINE PLANTS TO MAKE A FRAME

In a garden where you aim to have more subtle combinations and greater variety, you can use several different plants to make a single frame. In doing this the designer relies on the mind's love of pattern. When no obvious pattern is in sight, our minds often concoct one. We look for similarities in what we see, associate related objects, and deal with what remains as exceptional. If you place a red plant on one side of the focal point and a red plant on the other side, we will see the area between the two reds as framed, even if the two red plants are quite different in all other characteristics. The same holds true for using similar shapes or similar textures on either side of the focal point. Although it may have been a struggle for you to consciously study plant shapes and textures as you made your plant list, it is natural for us to recognize patterns when we see them.

To help you understand subtle pattern making and frames, compare moviegoers with movie critics. The average person who sees a movie forms an opinion: liked it, didn't like it. He or she is not required to make an in-depth analysis of what led to this opinion. The movie critic will explain which factors — editing, directing, acting, etc. — contributed to the film's success or failure. Those who want to make a movie can learn from such critical analysis. Similarly, you can compare garden lovers with garden designers. Those who simply like to look at gardens appreciate pleasing plant combinations. No time need be spent trying to articulate the reasons. For the garden designer, understanding why certain plant groups are pleasing helps in creating more groups that please.

So experiment with subtle frames: a hosta flanked by the grassy forms of a sedge and a tradescantia; threadleaf coreopsis *(Coreopsis verticillata)* underlined with spiky carpet snapdragons

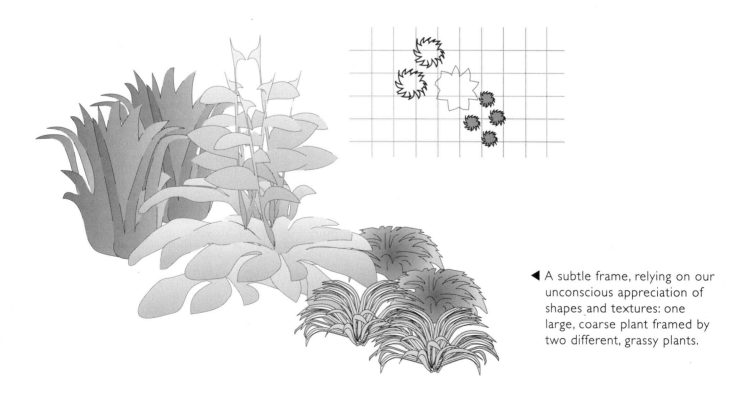

◀ A subtle frame, relying on our unconscious appreciation of shapes and textures: one large, coarse plant framed by two different, grassy plants.

Here's a look at four possible focal points and frames. They are shown as they would appear on a scale drawing and in a front view.

▲ A spike-flowered plant is framed all around by a lower, finer, mounded plant.

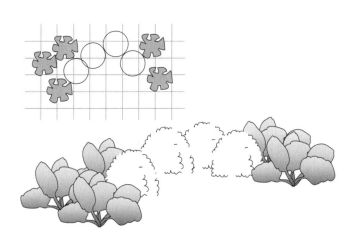

▲ A mounded plant is framed to the right and left with coarser plants.

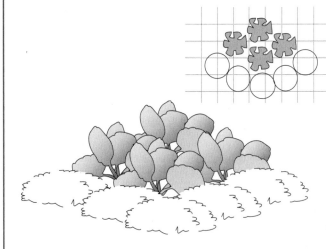

▲ This coarse plant's frame is an underline of low, fine plants.

▲ The difference between a plant and its framing plants can be more or less dramatic. Here, a coarse plant is framed by a background of a second coarse plant.

(*Antirrhinum majus* 'Floral Carpet')
and backed by spiky false dragonshead
(*Physostegia virginica*); dwarf astilbe
(*Astilbe chinensis pumila*) flanked by
blue creeping forget-me-not (*Myosotis
scorpioides*) on one side and great blue
lobelia (*Lobelia siphilitica*) on the other.

FORMAL AND
INFORMAL FRAMES

The shape and composition of
frames should be in keeping with the
style you chose for your garden, formal
or informal. A uniform circle of plants
around your focal point is more formal
than an oval, an irregular island, or a
broken line. But a regular circle can exist
within an informal garden, and an irregular shape can exist in a formal bed. It is
the repetition of certain elements, or
lack of repetition, more than any one
frame or group of plants, that creates the
overall formal or informal impression.

So take a mental step back to your main
viewpoint as you put frames around
your focal point. Look for obvious symmetry and repetition in a formal garden,
less symmetry and more variable patterns in an informal one. (For examples,
see below and page 104.)

Notice that the plants in these
drawings are not identified. As a
designer, it's up to you to picture plant
groups composed of shapes and textures. After the picture is in your mind,
decide which plants on your list will
create that picture. If your list lacks the
plant to finish the picture you envi-
sioned, go back to Step 5 and add some
plants to that list. The difference will be
that when you research plants now, you
have additional criteria: "The plant
must not only grow well on this site and
serve some goal of the garden, it must
be coarse textured and round" or "I
need a tall, columnar, fine-textured
plant" and so on.

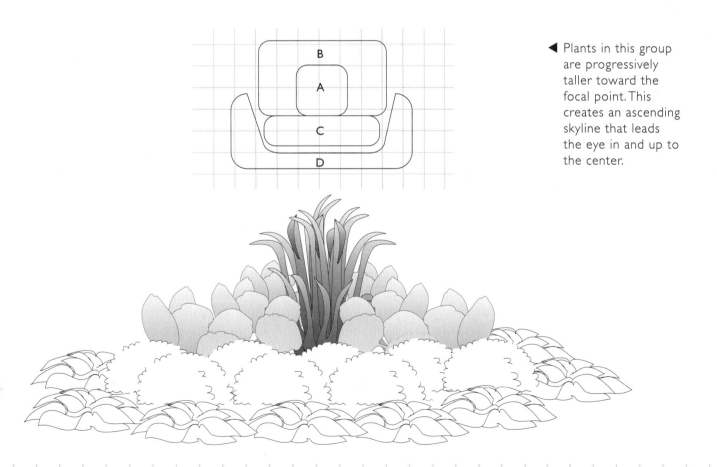

◀ Plants in this group
are progressively
taller toward the
focal point. This
creates an ascending
skyline that leads
the eye in and up to
the center.

▶ There is a formal
feeling to this focal
point (A) and its
frames (B, C, D).

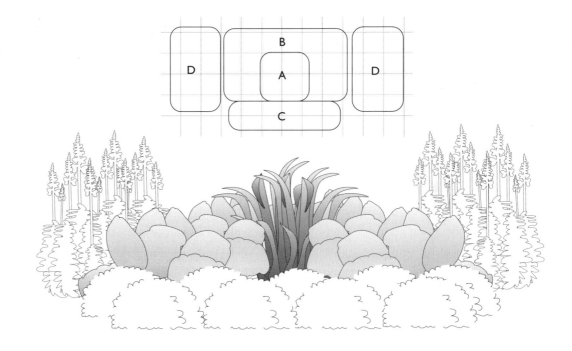

▶ The same or similar
plants as those
illustrated above can
be grouped informally,
as shown here.

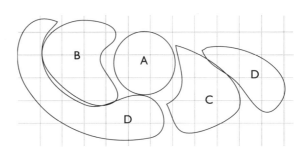

Leading the Eye with Lines You Create

Every group of plants has an edge. We see edges as lines. Remember what powerful tools lines are in leading the eye. We can manipulate the lines we make with groups of plants so that they guide the viewer's gaze within the garden or landscape.

Sometimes we follow lines with our eyes, sometimes with our minds, sometimes with our feet. The road that winds away to the horizon is a well-known artist's device to help draw a viewer's eye through a painting. That path through the painting doesn't have to be solid, it can appear and disappear. The viewer follows the path mentally and is pleased to see it reappear where expected, intrigued or disturbed to see it in an unexpected place. An actual path through a garden can prompt visitors to follow the line with their feet, a reward for the designer who aimed to encourage exploration.

As you place frames around the focal point, think about where you want the garden bed to go. If your focal point is in the center of the area you envision as garden, your frames can lead the eye equally to left and right. If your focal point is to one side of the area, you can use your frame lines to point toward the far side of the garden. For examples, see page 106.

▶ Frames in this group stretch out toward the right, creating a long, gentle slope to lead the eye.

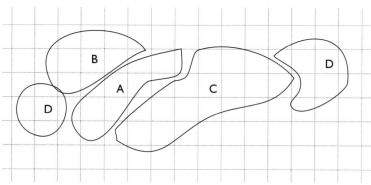

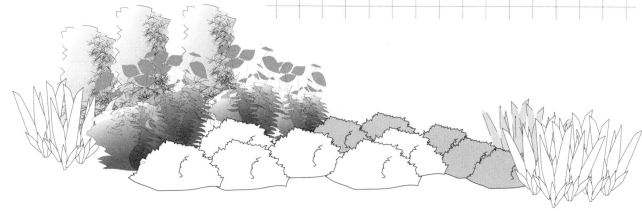

▶ The B frame in this group creates a low path that pulls the eye through and around to the back of the garden.

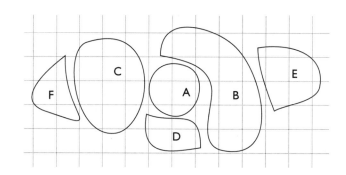

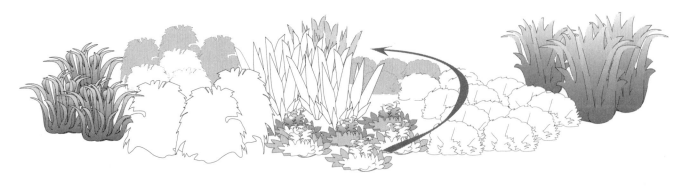

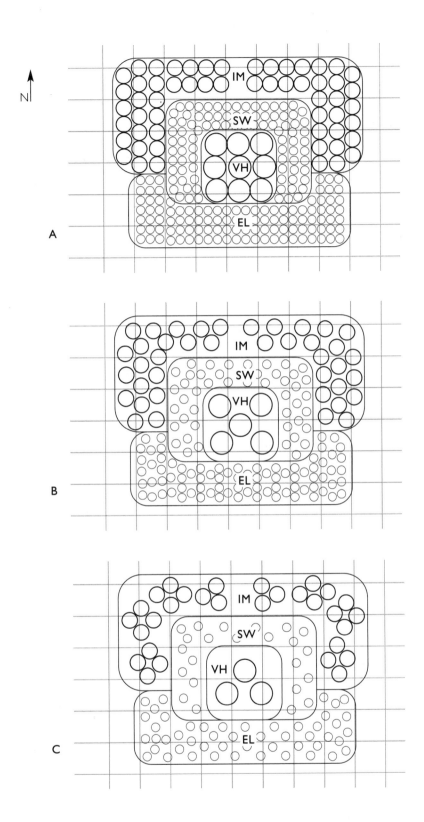

N

A

B

C

◀ Numbers of plants in each focal point or frame can be varied to fit a budget.
(A) In this 16 sq. ft. bed, 262 plants for the "can't wait" gardener: 9 hosta, 89 woodruff, 108 lobelia, 56 impatiens.
(B) In the same bed, 171 plants for the gardener who can wait a month or so: 5 hosta, 46 woodruff, 80 lobelia, 40 impatiens. Perennial numbers were reduced more than annuals, since they can continue to fill next season.
(C) Finally, 102 plants for the gardener who can wait for plants to grow to their full spread: 3 hosta, 22 woodruff, 47 lobelia, 30 impatiens. Again, perennial numbers were reduced more than annuals.

Key to Plant Names
VH - Variegated hosta: perennial, nice foliage all summer, lilac flowers in July, 12–18"

SW - Sweet woodruff: perennial, spring-green foliage, white flowers in May, 8"

EL - Edging lobelia: annual, trailing habit, dark blue flowers all summer, 6" mat of dark green foliage

IM - Impatiens: annual, pink, white, and red flowers all summer, 18–24" mounds

Spacing Plants

I have been showing you outlines of frames and focal points, without individual plants drawn into those outlines. You should try to design the same way. Concern yourself first with where you want a certain type of plant to appear and how much area the plants must cover. Only then should you draw individual plants into that area. Figure individual plants to fit your budget, not plant group placement. The drawings on page 107 show the same combination of focal point and frames, with individual plants drawn in to meet different goals and budgets.

All those plant symbols on page 107 would be tedious to draw. In this book it was done only to illustrate this point. It's only necessary to draw in every single plant in the design when precise placement is critical. Most of the time you can indicate plant quantities in other ways. Just figure the number of square feet the species will occupy and use a chart such as the one below to arrive at numbers of plants. (I covered the pluses and negatives of crowding in

the last step. Now this chart gives you my definition of "crowded.")

This is my own personal plant spacing chart. You can use it if you don't have one of your own, but you should know that some people will disagree with the numbers here. For instance, nowhere on my chart will you find numbers approaching the plant density common in front of many greenhouses and nurseries. Nurseries have the plants at hand and an urgent need to make instant advertising displays. It's a shame that so many people, including landscapers, copy this technique even though the underlying need is not there. Such close spacing in most places is simply a waste of plants and money.

I realize this may sound eccentric, but for now, give me the benefit of the doubt. It could save you some money in the future. Next spring, visit a botanical garden and observe the spacious arrangement of annual bedding plants there. Those same beds will get "oohs" and "ahs" all summer, but they're barren wastelands in spring, compared to the average nursery's bedding display. Don't think this is because the botanical gar-

Plant Spacing	For the Hurried Gardener: Crowded Spacing*	For Those Who Can Wait: One-Season Fill*	If There's No Rush: Wide Spacing
Annual, 10–12" spread	4–5 per sq. ft.	2 per sq. ft.	1 per sq. ft.
Annual, 12–18" spread	2–3 per sq. ft.	1–2 per sq. ft.	0.7–1 per sq. ft.
Annual, 18–24" spread	2 per sq. ft.	0.7–1 per sq. ft.	0.5 per sq. ft.
Perennial, 6–12" spread	2–3 per sq. ft.	2 per sq. ft.	1 or less per sq. ft.
Perennial, 12–18" spread	1–2 per sq. ft.	1 per sq. ft.	0.7 or less per sq. ft.
Perennial, 24" + spread	1 per sq. ft.	0.7 per sq. ft.	0.5 or less per sq. ft.

*There's a price to pay for crowding. More plants per square foot means increased demand on the soil for water and nutrients. Crowded plants are also more susceptible to attack by diseases and pests, particularly fungus and mildew. A perennial plant's shape can be ruined and its flowering reduced. The caretaker must supply the extra attention needed if crowding is to pay off.

den can't afford additional plants. Botanical gardens that do have a little more to spend still don't crowd a space with baby plants. They grow or buy the same quantity of older, larger plants! Go back to the botanical gardens four weeks after your first visit and see for yourself how nicely those plants are filling in. They'll be glorious all summer. Meanwhile, at the nursery, that crowded bed will be pulled apart and replanted several times as the plants wear out or sale items change.

Since we're on the subject of saving money, when we have to reduce plant cost, let's do it without looking cheap. Here's a way to cut the number of plants in half without doubling the space between each pair of plants: Group the plants to leave more space between frames, less space between individual plants. This way the illusion of fullness is maintained.

Completing the Focal Point

Frame the focal point until placing more frames would not suit your site, budget, or reasons for the garden. If the area you have to work with is restricted, you may decide to stop framing when there is not enough room to the left or behind the focal point to complete another frame. If you have a larger area but a requirement for variety in the garden, you may decide to stop when the frames become so large that the next frame would tie up too much room in a single plant species. Usually two or three frames are enough to make whatever is in the focal point stand out clearly in any garden or yard.

A single focal point and its frames can be a complete garden or a portion of a garden. The reasons for the garden, the site, and the budget will tell you which way to proceed. A garden meant

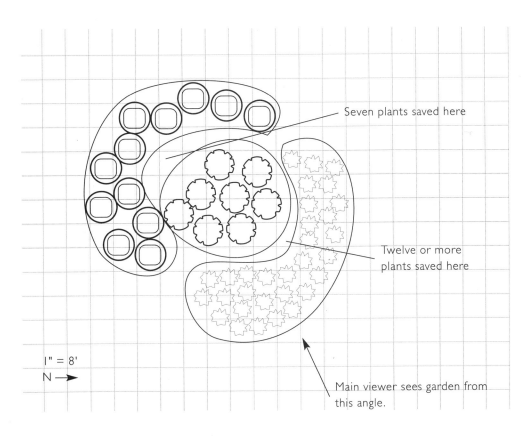

Seven plants saved here

Twelve or more plants saved here

Main viewer sees garden from this angle.

1" = 8'
N →

◀ Spaces left between groups of plants are not apparent to the viewer and do not appear to be part of the design. Unplanted space can be attractive, highlighting each plant group. This can also be an effective technique for reducing plant cost.

for distant viewing may have to consist of a single focal point with three frames, or its pattern would not be visible. That garden might consist of hundreds of individual plants.

In a garden meant to be seen close by — for instance, one that must highlight a birdbath — and to be completed inexpensively, there may again be only a single focal point and three frames. The important difference is that this garden would be planted with just three dozen plants in all.

A single focal point group would probably not work if the garden is meant to showcase a variety of plants. Such a garden would probably have five or six separate focal point groups.

Moving On

If your garden design goals are best met with a single focal point and frames, you're almost done. Skip Step 10 and go on to Step 11.

If your garden should have additional focal points and you have no budget constraints, go on to Step 10.

If you are feeling pinched when it comes to budget but want to add more focal points, consider this before going on: A garden can be planted in stages. The design recipe in this book lends itself well to phased-in gardens. With some help from the designer, the gardener can simply construct the garden in the same sequence it was designed. Each focal point and its frames can be an independent garden, pleasing on its own yet ready for expansion to include the next stage. In a phased-in garden you can even take advantage of this money-saving technique: Repeat some perennial plants throughout the garden. Plants from earlier stages can then be divided for planting later stages. In the space below, sketch your focal point and frames, indicating the number of plants that you think are required for your particular needs.

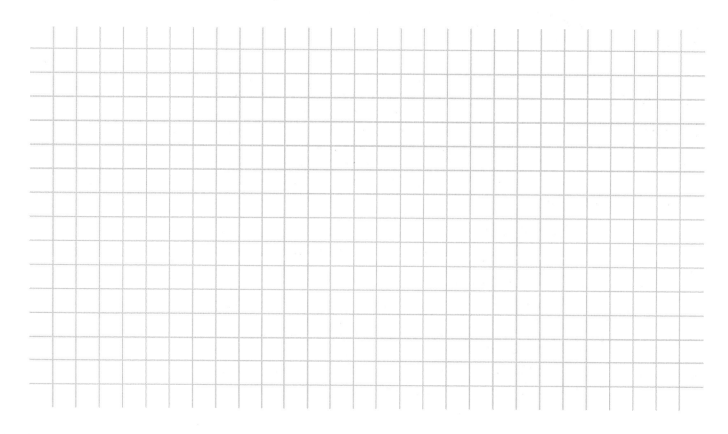

Add to the Basic Plan

The tenth step to successful landscape design is to add more groups of plants to the garden. Each new group is composed in the same manner as the primary focal point and its frames. These secondary focal points can be arranged to lead the viewer's eye around the garden or to highlight the primary focal point and its frames. Or, they may be designed to serve both of these purposes.

Setting Up a Visual Tour

The most interesting gardens offer a self-guided tour, where interest flows from one area to another throughout the entire garden. Mentally step back and look at the plan you have so far. Think of the first focal point and its frames as a focal point group. Once you have the viewer's attention on the first focal point group, where would you like the viewer's eye to be drawn next? Imagine the focal point group as a single peak on the horizon. You're about to add more peaks and create valleys. These new peaks can flow smoothly or abruptly from the first one, calmly, or in a dramatic, exciting way.

Pick a spot for a second focal point group. For the smoothest, calmest flow, allow enough room between each focal point group so that at least one frame separates the second focal point plant from the first group. If a more abrupt change is in keeping with the feel of your garden, the second focal point can be placed immediately adjacent to the outer frame of the first focal point.

Plot the second focal point but don't select the plant or frame it yet. Look at the overall plan. Will you be placing even more focal points? If so, pick the spots for those other focal points right now. Additional focal points will help lead the eye in a tour through the garden.

Additional focal points can also create a line that points the viewer to an attractive feature outside the garden.

When you plot the dot-to-dot path through the garden, a line is created. Remember that the line can contribute to the feeling of the garden. A symmetrical ring of focal point groups is more formal than one that meanders through the garden.

KEEP THE SPOTLIGHT ON THE FIRST FOCAL POINT GROUP

If the first focal point in your garden is important enough to the design that its spotlight should always be brighter than any other, that can be arranged as you set up additional focal points. These secondary focal point groups can be arranged to frame the first focal point. Again, you can influence the feeling of your garden with the placement and composition of the additional focal point groups.

The relationship between plants in different focal point groups can also affect the overall impact of the garden. Repeating elements from the first focal point group throughout the garden can be a unifying theme. Study the example of how repeated elements can unify focal points at the top of page 114.

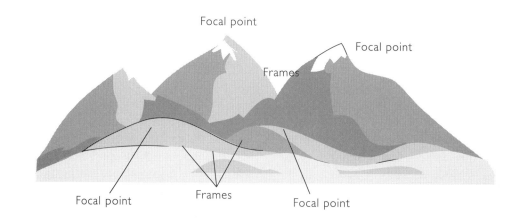

▶ Think of the garden as a natural vista: Focal points are hills or peaks, frames are valleys. In this design, rocky peaks make an exciting transition, while rolling hills make a calm transition.

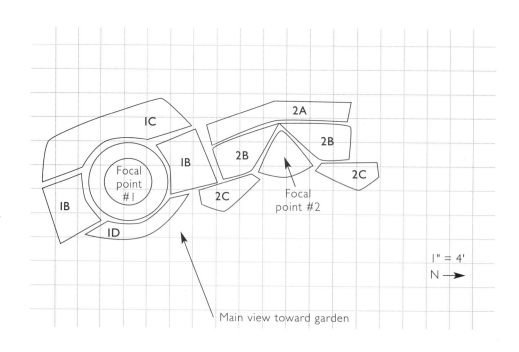

▶ Placing one or more frames between focal point plants gives the viewer time to take in one focal point group before being drawn into the next. In this calm, "rolling hills" design, several frames separate the two focal point plants.

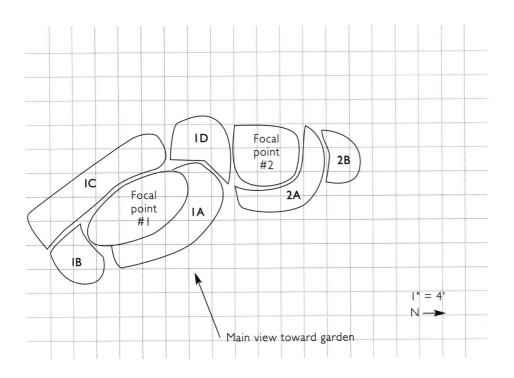

IC

ID

Focal
point
#2

2B

Focal
point
#1

IA

2A

IB

1" = 4'
N →

Main view toward garden

◀ Here, the second focal
point is adjacent to the D
frame of the first focal
point group. The viewer's
gaze slides down the
valley of frames around
the first focal point and
comes abruptly to the
next "peak" in the
garden's topography.

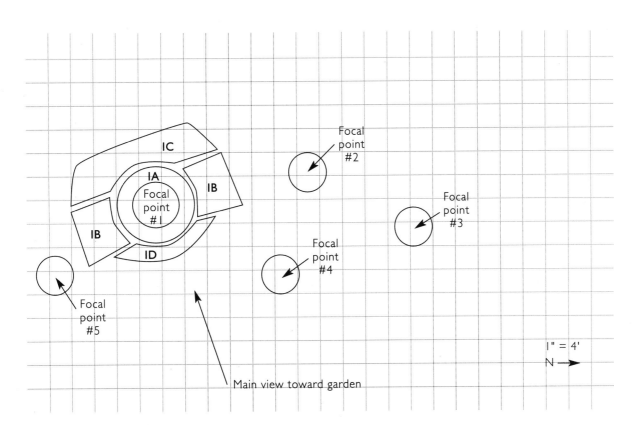

IC

Focal
point
#2

IA
Focal
point
#1

IB

Focal
point
#3

IB

ID

Focal
point
#4

Focal
point
#5

Main view toward garden

1" = 4'
N →

▲ From the first focal point the eye will follow the flow to the next point and so on
throughout the garden. The designer determines the flow when placing secondary
focal points.

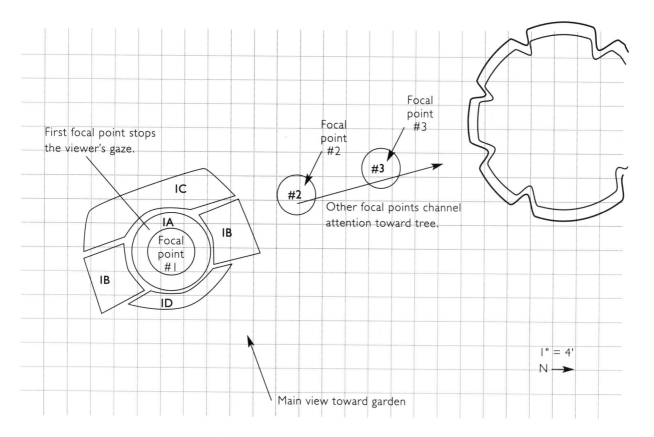

First focal point stops the viewer's gaze.

IC

IA

Focal point #1

IB

IB

ID

Focal point #2

#2

Focal point #3

#3

Other focal points channel attention toward tree.

I" = 4'

N →

Main view toward garden

▲ You can line up the focal points to lead the viewer's eye to some attractive object, such as an ornamental tree, a second garden, a lovely point on the horizon, and so on.

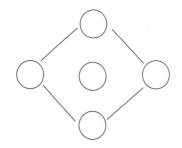

Formal arrangements of focal points

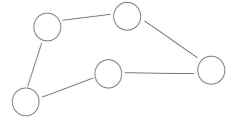

Less formal arrangements of focal points

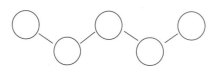

▲ Primary and secondary focal points can create a symmetrical, formal pattern or a free-form, informal pattern.

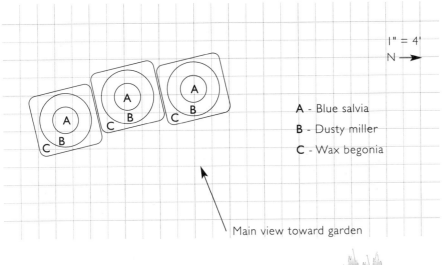

1" = 4'
N →

A - Blue salvia
B - Dusty miller
C - Wax begonia

Main view toward garden

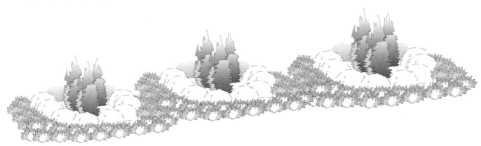

◀ The most formal garden has identical plant arrangements at each focal point. If a slightly less formal look is desired, flanking areas A could be planted with a pyramidal plant different from that used in the central section A. The flanking areas B and C could also be filled with plants similar but not identical to the plants in the middle B and C.

1" = 4'
N →

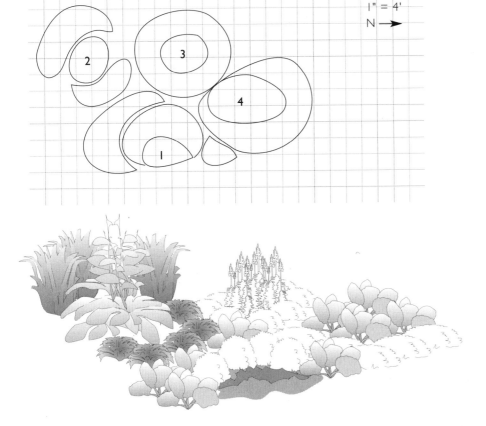

◀ In this informal design, secondary focal points 2, 3, and 4 form a background frame for #1. Secondary focal point plants are arranged in an informal arc, in descending order of height. This garden could be even more informal if focal point plants 2, 3, and 4 were not in height order. Formality could be increased by making focal point plants 2, 3, and 4 more alike: for example, all red, all grassy textured, and so on.

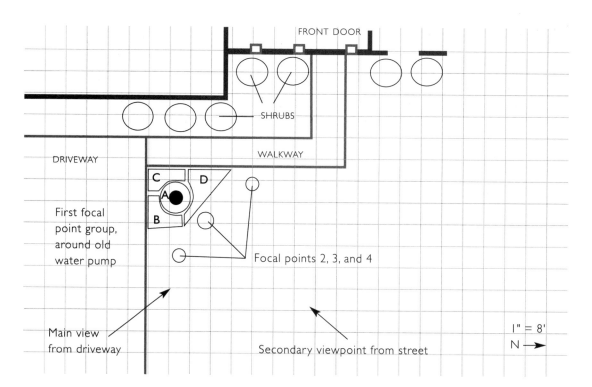

FRONT DOOR

SHRUBS

DRIVEWAY

WALKWAY

C   D

A ●

B

First focal
point group,
around old
water pump

Focal points 2, 3, and 4

Main view
from driveway

Secondary viewpoint from street

1" = 8'

N →

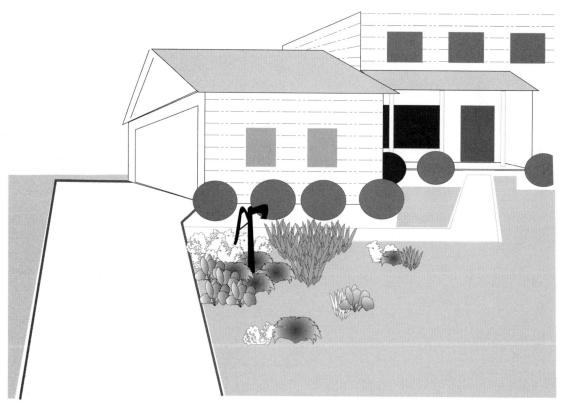

▲ Several secondary focal points are planned to lead the viewer
toward the front door. To add a formal touch and unity, plants from
the first focal point group will be repeated throughout the bed, in
varying combinations.

PAMPER THE MAIN VIEWER

The lines you create by connecting focal points can also make the main viewer more comfortable. Pamper the main viewer, make that person feel as if the garden is a stage and his own position is front row, center.

Think about the seating arrangements in theaters, and you will never forget how to do this. Seats are arranged parallel to the edge of the stage or in a semicircle with its radius at center stage.

When the lines you've drawn through the garden with your focal points are oriented as if they outline a stage for your main viewer, the viewer feels like an honored guest: The garden performance is obviously meant just for his or her pleasure.

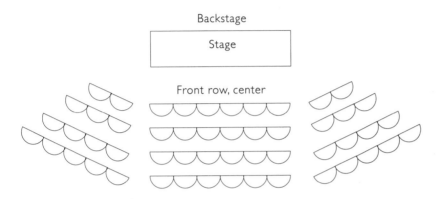

◀ Keep theater seating in mind as you lay out the garden. The best theater seats are squared off to the front of the stage; the best garden is squared off to the main viewer.

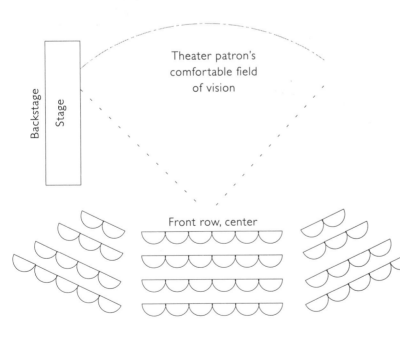

◀ The seats in this imaginary theater are arranged awkwardly. Viewers in the front row would have to twist their bodies to "enjoy" the performance. Although this arrangement in a theater seems ludicrous, many people put up with it in gardens!

Working with Predetermined Garden Outlines

There shouldn't be an outline around the garden yet. Back in Step 6 when we selected a focal point, I asked you to hold off on this. But also in Step 6 I mentioned that there are some situations where the overall shape of the garden is cast in stone, as when the garden area is outlined by patio, walkways, and house. If the garden has a predetermined shape, and that shape has a long axis that faces away from the viewer, what can you do to create a center-stage feeling? Simple. Have the "cast" turn to face the viewer. It's not as easy to arrange plants this way, where width is so restricted, but it does work.

Don't create this awkward situation for yourself. Avoid following lot lines, walls, or walkways with your plant groups unless this makes sense for your main viewer. The drawings below and on the opposite page show two common situations in which the designer may fall into the "misaligned stage" trap. You should be able to recognize or correct for these pitfalls now.

When the plants are all arranged within the garden area, and you're happy with the frames and lines you've drawn, it's time to outline the bed. If you've waited until now to decide on an outline for your garden, you made a wise move!

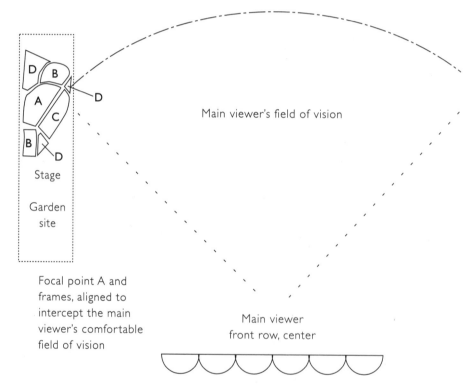

Focal point A and frames, aligned to intercept the main viewer's comfortable field of vision

▲ Occasionally, you may have to design a garden in a predetermined area where that area is turned away from the main viewer. Remember, in gardens as in theaters, if the stage isn't turned toward the paying customers, the plants/actors must turn to face the audience.

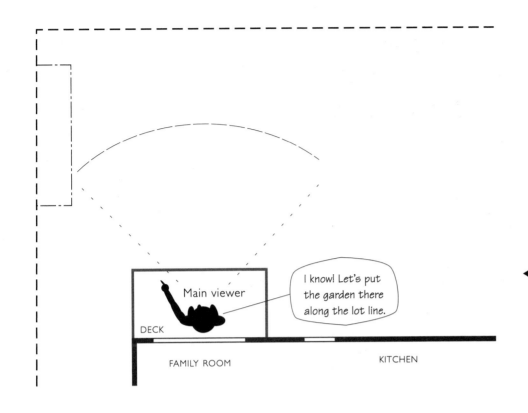

Since we can easily recognize a misaligned stage, it's amazing that we set up that same situation with our gardens.

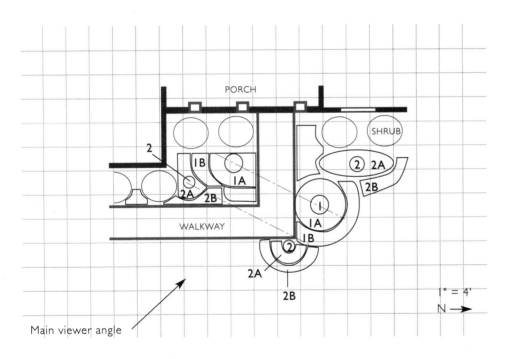

Straight-line objects such as walls and fences may fool you into turning the stage away from your viewer. The tendency here may be to put the A plants flanking the door at the top of the walk. But think about the viewer. The same frame can be created, turned toward the main viewer, and still look good from other angles.

▶ Sketch out several possible focal point areas ("stages") here. Be sure to indicate the main viewer angle, as well as any secondary viewpoints.

Outline the Garden

The eleventh step to successful landscape design is to give the garden an overall shape. Look at the arrangement of focal point groups to find a suggested irregular outline for the bed or use a specific shape, such as a square or circle. Use the outline you prefer, modifying it as needed to preserve the effect that the plant groups already create.

Using Focal Points as a Guide

The outline of the garden should be a logical extension of everything the designer has done to this stage. The pattern created by focal points in the garden can be used to develop an outline. The outline that results may be anything from a formal circle to an informal free-form shape. It will match the feeling of the garden.

Imagine the garden as a dot-to-dot drawing just waiting for a pencil line to connect everything. The focal points are the dots. Connect them. Look at the shape that results. That shape could be enlarged and used to surround the entire garden.

Experiment with different shapes:

- If secondary focal points have been arranged to frame the first focal point group, you may choose to disregard the central focal point in the dot-to-dot drawing.
- If your secondary focal points and your main focal point create a line to draw the viewer's eye through the garden, you can connect those focal points. They may create a line you can use as the viewer's edge of the garden.
- For the garden that has only one focal point and its frames, a line that can simply encompass all of the frames is a good outline.
- In the garden that frames a background feature, an edge that will enhance that purpose makes very good sense.

Avoid Motion Sickness

As you draw the garden outline, keep it simple: free of excessive dips and curves. The edge of a bed is a very strong line and draws a lot of attention. Imagine the viewer taking a visual trip around the bed edge. Every place the bed edge slips into a bay or juts out to a peninsula calls for special notice. A few side trips are pleasant; when there are too many they can be tedious detours.

TRY CIRCLES, SQUARES, OR RECTANGLES

There are a number of reasons that lead to making a regular outline for the garden, even an irregularly shaped garden. The garden may back up to a building, straight lot line, or walkway that calls for at least one straight edge. Some people prefer to see their gardens entirely contained within straight lines and right angles. Others prefer to edge their gardens, and the materials to be used as an edge aren't conducive to free-form curves.

▶ These focal points create an irregular diamond shape that can be enlarged to encompass the whole garden. For those who prefer curves to sharp angles, the corners can be rounded off.

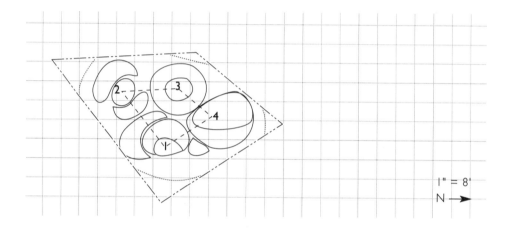

1" = 8'
N →

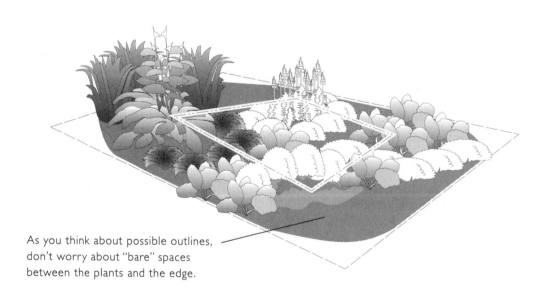

As you think about possible outlines, don't worry about "bare" spaces between the plants and the edge.

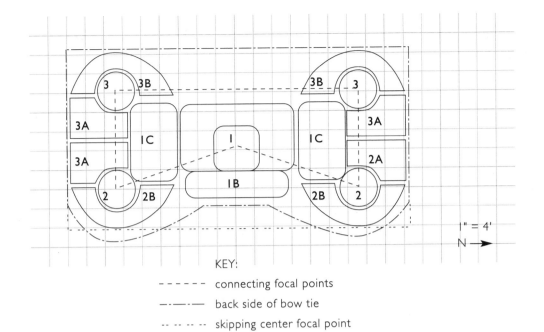

KEY:

– – – – – connecting focal points

—·—·— back side of bow tie

·· – ·· – ·· skipping center focal point

1" = 4'

N →

◀ Connecting the focal points in this formal garden makes a bow tie shape. If the garden is meant to be seen only from the front (bottom of this drawing), the back side of the bow tie can be straightened out. If a bow tie or one-sided bow tie doesn't suit you, try skipping the center, main focal point. This creates a rectangle.

You're the artist. You can give the garden the shape that you like or that suits the site. Going back to the analogy of the garden designer as a painter: You've finished your garden painting and are now ready to have it framed. There are many standard shapes to choose from. Any of them can be used, since the shape of the outline will not change the picture within, it will simply be the frame for that picture.

Think about a portrait, matted with an oval mat and framed in a rec-tangular frame. It's an attractive tech-nique. Why was it done that way? Maybe the framer didn't have any oval frames to work with. Maybe a combina-tion of shapes was chosen purposely for its effect: For example, the portrait is surrounded by four matching triangles. The point is, you have as much artistic license as that framer. If there is a reason to make the overall bed square, rectan-gular, or any other regular shape, you can do it. You may not even need to rearrange the plants in the bed.

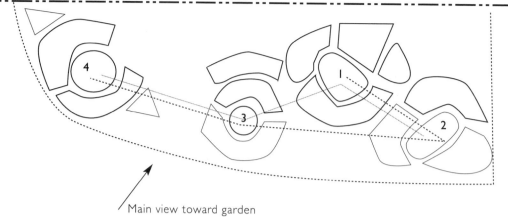

Lot line

Main view toward garden

▲ Here, four focal points are arranged to conduct a tour through the garden. They can be connected dot-to-dot at least two ways. You can choose one of the lines that results for the viewer's edge of the garden.

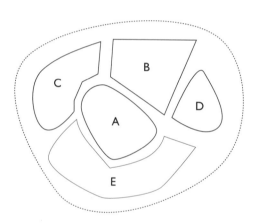

◀ A garden can be outlined in any shape that encompasses all the frames. Keep the outline as simple as possible. Don't be concerned about the bare space.

EMPTY SPACE IS OKAY

Notice the empty spaces between some of the plants and the edge, in the drawing above. Don't rush back to your plant list and begin plugging in more plants. Think again of the portrait with the oval matte and rectangular frame. You probably don't feel any urge to paste additional photos into the empty spaces around that portrait. Treat any empty spaces between your edge and your plants as if the whole garden was that framed portrait. There is always the option to leave them unplanted.

Ah, but we sometimes do fill the corners of that oval-in-a-rectangle por-

trait, you may think. Correct: That's another option you have. Consider what might appear in the corners of that portrait. Take your cues from successful artistic work of all kinds. If identical flourishes in each corner create a look that would be in keeping with the style of this garden, then the unplanted space between your carefully arranged plants and the bed edge could also be handled in a uniform fashion. You can use a mat-forming plant or an attractive mulch, either of which can flow around the edges of all the plant groups to create an attractive feature that actually unifies the bed.

If the main viewer is some distance from the garden and the visual impact of the overall garden is already "just so," unplanted space should be handled in a low-key fashion. It can be filled with plants that are not meant to be seen from afar as separate elements, but to be admired up close. Low-visibility plants that can work in these spaces include plants with cool-color flowers, such as blue and purple. Cool colors tend to appear only as dark shadows when seen from a distance. Another possibility is to use a variety of plants that are attractive together but whose differences are subtle enough to make them blend together from a distance. Plants that can be admired by the close viewer without altering the image seen by the distant viewer can add dimension to the garden.

EDGING MATERIALS

Give some thought to what kind of material could make the edge of the garden. The edge of the garden can be constructed of a number of materials or consist simply of clean-cut sod. Wood, flexible plastic, strips of metal, rock, or brick might outline the garden. Each offers a different look. Some can also serve to reduce maintenance, and you know best whether your caretaker needs your help with this.

The edging used on the garden can tie the bed into the yard. If a brick patio is adjacent, a matching brick edge can be attractive. If foundation beds are edged with wood, the garden edge can repeat that detail. Rock edging can be very pretty in the yard if the house has fieldstone walls, but rocks can appear to be out of place if there are no others anywhere in sight.

List possible filler plants here:

List possible edging materials here:

Treat any empty spaces between your edge and your plants as if the whole garden were a framed portrait. It's up to you to either leave the spaces empty or fill them in.

▶ No edge is needed along the walkway and driveway. Connecting the secondary focal points suggests a dimpled edge along the lawn side of the garden. This edge enhances the line of focal points (3, 2, 3) that leads the main viewer's eye toward the front door.

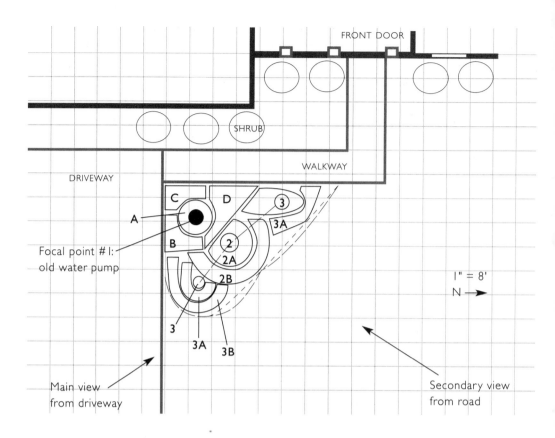

▶ You may decide that the dimpled edge creates too much attention on focal point 2, when seen by the secondary viewer. If you want the line of focal points and the bed edge to point the secondary viewer toward the front door, you can straighten out the dimple.

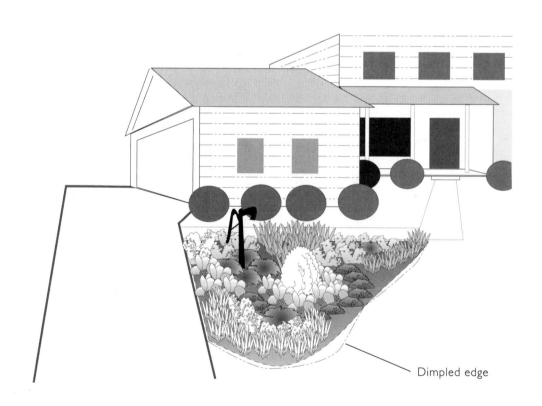

Garden edges that extend below ground level act as root barriers, keeping surrounding roots out of the garden and keeping garden plants confined. How invasive are the competing plants in the area of this garden: grass, suckering shrubs, vines? Is there a likelihood the garden plants will escape into and mar the look of the lawn? If a root barrier is desirable, check how deep the roots of competing plants grow around the bed or how deep invasive garden plant roots will be. The edge should be at least as deep as competing or invading plant roots.

Be specific with any choice of edging material: the purpose it serves, material it should be, and depth to which it should extend.

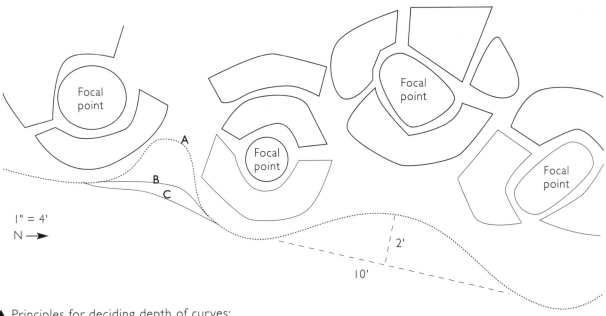

▲ Principles for deciding depth of curves:
- Dips in the bed edge shouldn't be deeper than they are wide, unless it's a very large bed, with curves 15 or 20 feet wide.
- Curves shouldn't pull the viewer's eye into a part of the garden unless it's an important part. Here, if the curve at "A" is a useful attention getter, it can remain, but be made less deep (B). It could also be eliminated (C) from the main viewer's perspective.

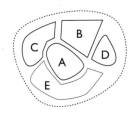 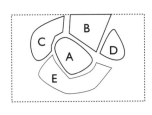 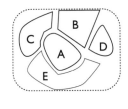 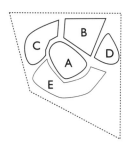

▲ There is no right or wrong outline for your planting beds.

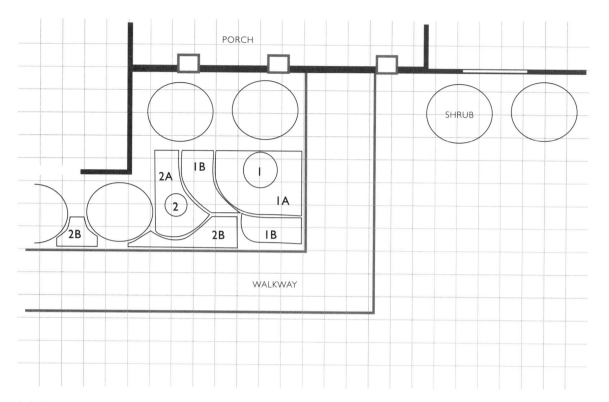

▲ Where the bed is surrounded by pavement and walls, you can decide to use those existing edges.

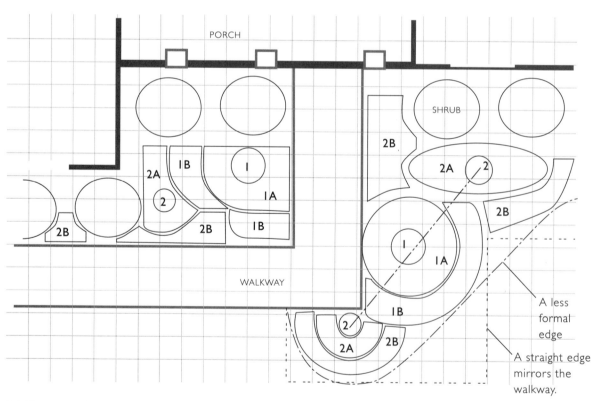

A less formal edge

A straight edge mirrors the walkway.

▲ When you choose to extend a successful garden outside the walkway, you can make a straight edge to match the walkway. Or, you may connect the focal points and choose a less formal edge.

Adjust before Planting

The twelfth step to successful landscape design is to take a final step back to the viewing points and imagine the plants as they appear on the design. Look at how the important plants and plant groups appear from each angle and whether their backgrounds are appropriate. Check that lines are leading the eye only to attractive features. Decide whether the scene is pleasantly balanced. Ask yourself whether you would enjoy maintaining this garden. Most importantly, determine whether the garden's goals have been met. You may find that all is well: You're done! Or you can make adjustments to correct lines, balance, and maintenance problems now, since changes and moves are much easier on paper than in a finished garden.

Assessing the Plan

Mentally walk around the garden. See if each focal point plant has a good background. You may decide to change or move a plant.

It takes only an eraser to make a change at this stage. In the example on the next page, the designer noticed that a purple flower would get lost in a background of dark foliage. The plant symbol or plant list indicated the important characteristics a replacement plant would need: height, shape, texture. A spiky, pink, 18-inch veronica (*Veronica spicata* 'Fox') would make a good substitute for the salvia. Simple: Erase salvia 'Blue Queen' from the key and replace it with veronica 'Fox'.

All that may be required to fix a poor background is some shifting of plants. In the example on page 131, the balloon flower (*Platycodon grandiflorus*) can suffer the fate of many blue flowers: When seen from a distance, the balloon flower could fade into the shadows or become lost in the purple coneflower (*Echinacea purpurea*) behind it. Some of the 'Silver King' artemisia plants are shifted from the secondary viewpoint so that gray foliage provides a contrasting backdrop for the balloon flower.

LINES POINT TWO WAYS

There is an old saying about never pointing a finger to accuse another, because in doing so you point four fingers back at yourself.

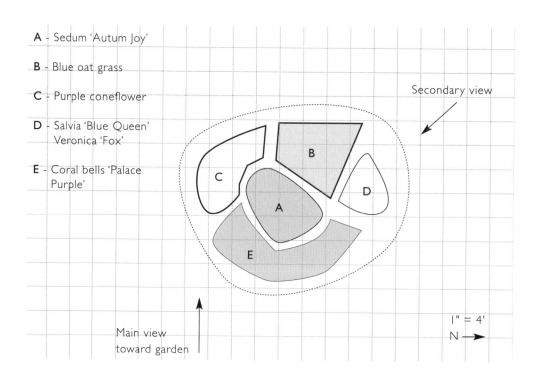

A - Sedum 'Autum Joy'

B - Blue oat grass

C - Purple coneflower

D - Salvia 'Blue Queen'
    Veronica 'Fox'

E - Coral bells 'Palace
    Purple'

Secondary view

Main view
toward garden

1" = 4'

N →

▶ Mentally walking around the garden, you see that from a secondary viewpoint plant D's blue-violet flowers line up with plant E, which has maroon foliage. The blue-violet flowers won't have a good background, so you go back to your plant list for an alternative to D or E. You find a veronica variety called 'Fox' that fits the bill: spiky, perennial, pink flowers that can be cut.

As you drew lines with groups of plants and edges, you created two-way streets. More than once I've found in checking different viewpoints that the edge of a bed that was carefully placed to show off some pretty sight instead spotlights a satellite dish, dilapidated shed, or other unattractive feature, as in the example on page 132.

Circle the garden, stopping at each place where people are likely to be looking at the garden. Look for any lines that stand out: bed edge, line of a particular plant, ascending row of plant tops. Let your eyes travel in the direction each line points, up toward the horizon, left or right. Then go to the next place where people will usually be when they see this garden and look along any of those same lines that pop out at you. The endpoints of those strong lines should be something worth seeing, not eyesores. The line that takes the main viewer's eye off into the woods may, from the far side of the garden, point back at the gas meter on the house. You can shift some plants to break up or redirect such lines.

CHECK BALANCE AND DISTRIBUTE WEIGHT

Imagine the garden area as if the whole scene is sitting on a large tray and that tray is resting on one palm of a server. Include on the tray all the important sights the viewer will be able to see without turning his or her head, such as the tree that is just right of the garden, the evergreen hedge to the left, and so on. Does the scene appear heavy in any direction? You can correct balance. Mass, color, texture, and seasonal interest all come into play.

Remember: The main viewer is still all-important. If the garden is very large and the viewer will be close to it, you may be weighing sections of the garden separately, since the viewer will not be seeing the entire garden all at one time.

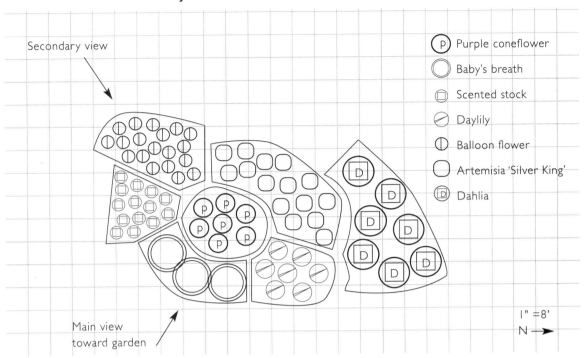

▲ Move from the main viewpoint around to the secondary viewpoint. Directly behind the balloon flower from that angle is purple coneflower; you want a background that offers more contrast.

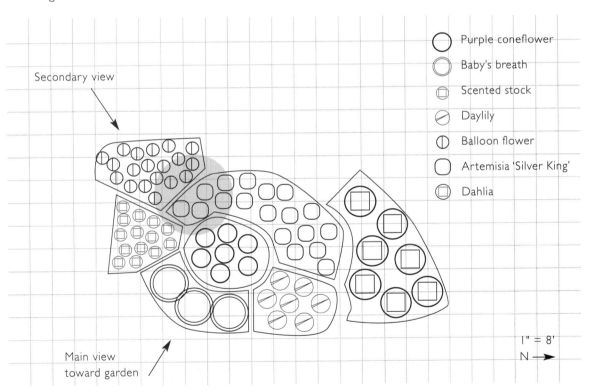

▲ A simple solution: Some gray artemisia 'Silver King' is shifted to act as a background for the balloon flower.

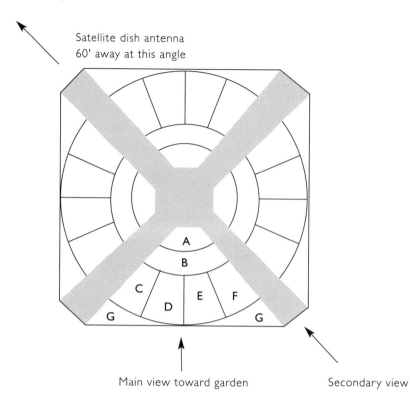

Satellite dish antenna
60' away at this angle

▶ Your formal,
symmetrical herb
garden design is nice
from the main viewer's
angle. But checking
from the secondary
viewpoint, you see that
the path will align the
viewer with the ugly
satellite dish in the
background.

Main view toward garden   Secondary view

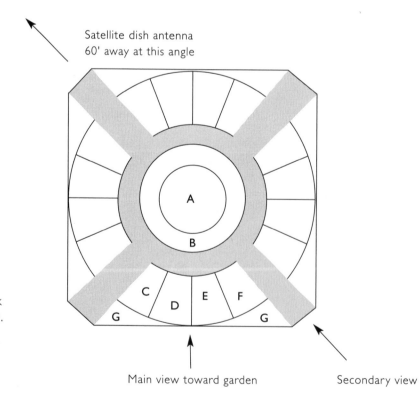

Satellite dish antenna
60' away at this angle

▶ You change the design
to include a central
planting that will break
up the line of the path.

Main view toward garden   Secondary view

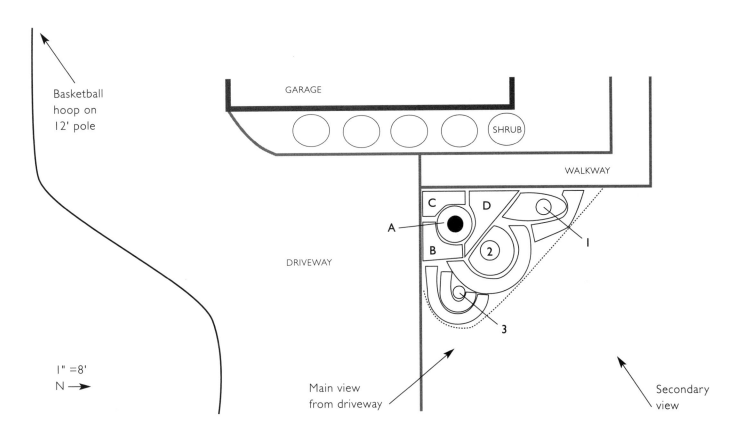

Basketball
hoop on
12' pole

GARAGE

SHRUB

WALKWAY

C   D

A ──●

B   2

I

3

DRIVEWAY

1" = 8'
N ──►

Main view
from driveway

Secondary
view

▲ Don't jump too quickly to make changes. Here, the 1–2 focal point line aims the
secondary viewer almost directly to a basketball hoop. But the viewer on this
street is usually moving, unlikely to focus on both the garden and its background
at the same time. So let it be!

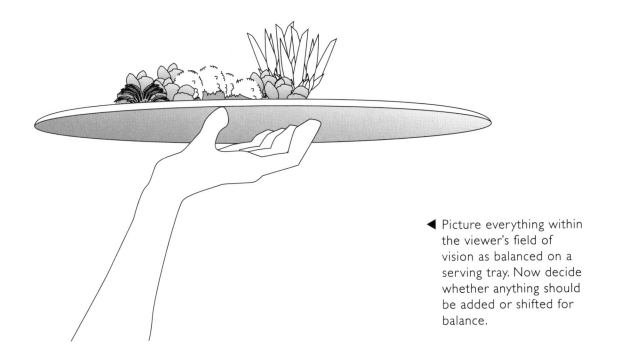

◄ Picture everything within
the viewer's field of
vision as balanced on a
serving tray. Now decide
whether anything should
be added or shifted for
balance.

MASSIVE ELEMENTS CAN BE BALANCED

A large mass such as a tree needs an equal mass to balance it. Although the tree is a vertical element, it doesn't necessarily need an identical vertical mass at the opposite end of the yard as a counterbalance. Features in a scene can balance just as two differently shaped children do on a teeter-totter. One short, stout child can balance a tall, lean child. One small child can move farther toward the end of the teeter-totter than the larger child on the opposite end, and balance results. The visual counterweight for the tree can be a horizontal feature of equal mass, such as a garden that reaches as far sideways as the tree reaches up. A rather small garden, in comparison to the tree, can balance the tree if the opposing garden is farther away from the center of the scene than the tree.

To correct for unbalanced masses, think about reducing or enlarging the garden or its counterweight, or shifting the location of the garden.

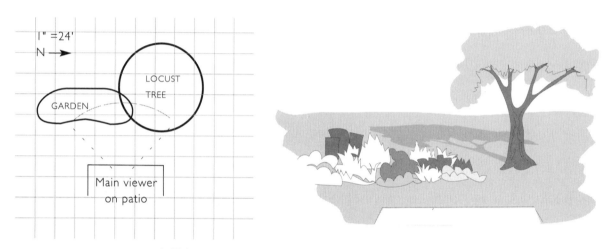

▲ This garden stretches to the left, balancing the vertical line of the tree with a long, horizontal line.

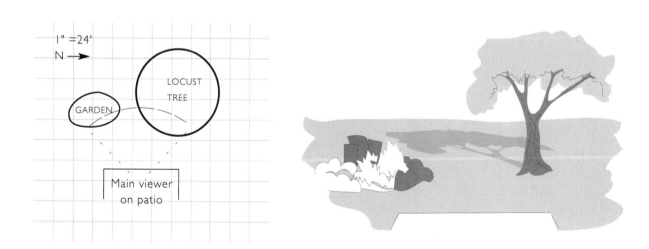

▲ A smaller garden can balance the same tree, if it is positioned farther to the left in the scene.

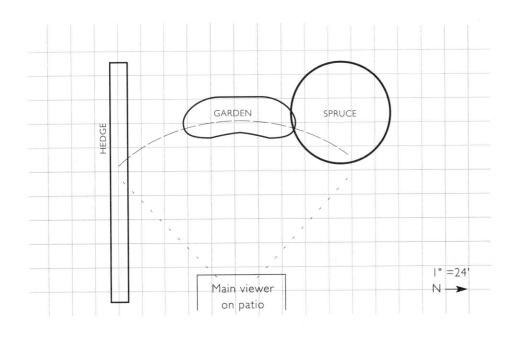

◀ Thirty-five feet from this garden, the main viewers see the spruce tree, the garden, and the hedge without turning their heads. Everything in that clear field of vision should be taken into account when it comes to balancing.

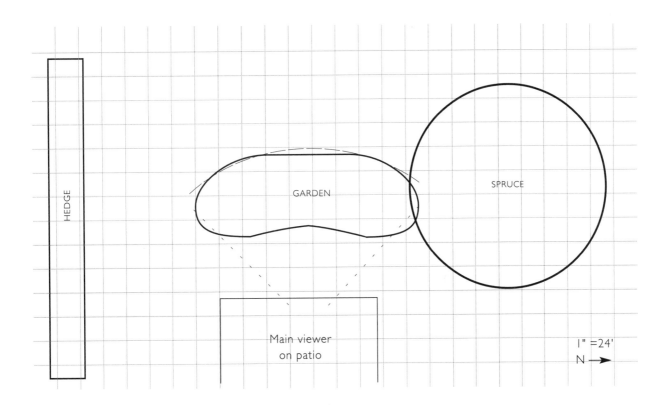

▲ If the main viewer is only 15 feet from the same garden shown above, the field of vision is almost entirely filled by garden. Things beyond the garden can be seen but are far enough away to require separate attention. The garden can be balanced without including the tree and hedge.

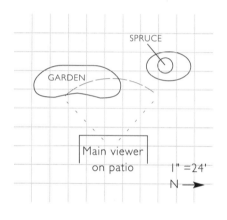

▲ This scene will be better balanced one day, when the spruce reaches its full 15- to 20-foot spread. For now, the spruce is too light to balance its side of the scene.

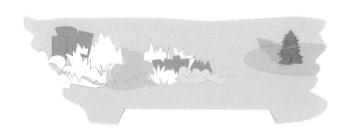

▲ Visual weight can be added via a large bed around the little spruce. Mulch or ground cover can fill the bed. Not only is the scene more balanced, but the tree will grow more quickly since you reduced root competition and mower damage.

DESIGN BASICS

Color and Texture Tip the Scales

Color and texture also have visual weight. Cool colors, such as blue and purple, tend to appear heavier to us than warm colors like red and yellow. Whites and pastels seem lighter yet. Fine plants strike us as heavier than coarse plants. If one half of the scene is filled entirely with warm colors and coarse texture, the other half with cool and fine, the design will appear unbalanced. A pocket of plants in the cool end of the garden can be replaced with warm color or coarse-textured varieties, sometimes without changing species. Just as with mass, this small group of plants, properly placed, can balance the whole end of a big garden.

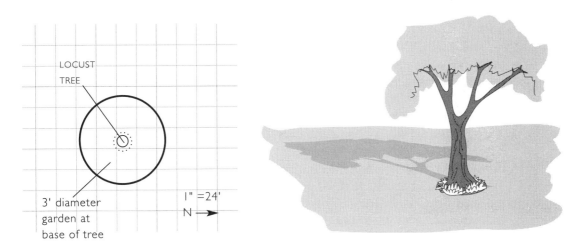

LOCUST
TREE

3' diameter
garden at
base of tree

1" =24'
N →

▲ A tiny flower bed at the base of a large
tree looks unbalanced.

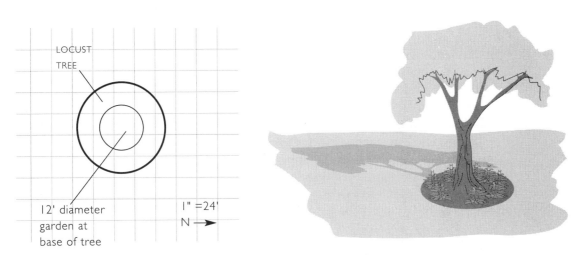

LOCUST
TREE

12' diameter
garden at
base of tree

1" =24'
N →

▲ Think about balancing the crown of the tree when
you put a garden at its feet. The tree will have a
solid visual base, and there will also be more
room to showcase the plants in the flower bed.

Make the Caretaker's Day

Look at the size of the garden and at your estimate of the caretaker's ability. Based on square footage and standard maintenance tasks alone, can the caretaker fit this garden's care into the schedule? Add time for plants that require extra care, such as tall delphiniums that will take 10 minutes every week to tie to their supporting stakes. If the garden requires more time than the caretaker can give,

explore the options. Can the garden be made smaller, be planted in stages, or consist of easier care plants? Could the caretaker be persuaded to spend extra time in the garden? You know the best course to take because you were there when the limit was set, in Step 3.

Even if the estimate you've made and the amount of time the caretaker's willing to spend match, check to see whether it's possible to make things simpler for the caretaker. Tips to simplify care will come mostly from your own experience, but you can also tap into the advice of others.

_____

_____

_____

_____

_____

_____

_____

_____

_____

_____

_____

_____

_____

_____

_____

_____

_____

_____

_____

_____

_____

_____

LEARN FROM THE PAST

It's likely that the maintenance problems you most despise will never bother the caretakers of gardens you design. That's because most gardeners learn enduring lessons from unpleasant maintenance tasks. When gardeners have struggled with unfriendly gardens, they probably constructed a mental list of plants and situations that will never again be included in their gardens. That is, if you've ever strained your back trying to weed far corners of a garden, you're likely to recognize the need for working paths that allow the caretaker to get right into the deepest parts of the garden. Or if you have fought deep-rooted, long-reaching quack grass or thistle for a season, you will probably always put deep root barriers around the garden if there are invasive plants nearby.

Be sure to think about weeding and watering. These two probably occupy more caretaker time than any other garden chores. See what you can do to simplify these things in this garden.

WEEDING

Deal with weeding first. It is possible to reduce weeding drastically by allowing desirable plants to totally fill all spaces or by using a mulch. Don't assume that even an experienced gardener knows what you know. Specify the material to be used for the mulch and the depth that should be maintained for weed control. My usual recommendation is an organic, small-particle material, such as processed bark or shredded leaves, to a 2-inch depth.

Weeding can't be eliminated entirely. Most people can comfortably weed areas up to 3 feet from where they are standing or kneeling. Island gardens more than 6 feet wide and one-sided gardens (those that back right up to a wall or fence) deeper than 3 feet should be scrutinized. Can all plants in this design be reached easily, or will the caretaker have to straddle plants to get into some areas? Give the caretaker places to stand so that all parts of the garden are within comfortable reach. This is as simple as pinching a frame here and there or slicing open the design to insert working paths.

Working paths should not be visual distractions. Angle working paths so that main viewers will not notice them.

Weeding can also create loads of debris. The caretaker must either be able to toss weeds a short distance to a clear spot for later disposal or safely navigate the garden with a basket or wheelbarrow. The more debris the gardener has to carry or wheel around, the wider the working paths must be.

WATERING

Then there's watering. Simple, you say, there's a sprinkler system. But is that big rotary sprinkler going to blast all the leaves off the plants in its path? Make a note to have it reset or add sprinklers to the zone. This is the kind of thing that makes experience so wonderful: I have worked around sprinkler systems enough that I can say with confidence, "Sprinklers are easier to adjust and change than you think."

Setting overhead sprinklers is something of an all-American pastime. Drive through your neighborhood some evening and watch people setting up sprinklers. Setting the sprinkler, turning it on, adjusting it, and readjusting it are dance steps. If the day is warm and the dancer is experienced and is dressed in gardening clothes, the music that goes with the dance may be a rather spritely march. But in other circumstances you are likely to see some unsettling contemporary ballet, complete with discordant sounds, abrupt changes in direction, and uneasy endings.

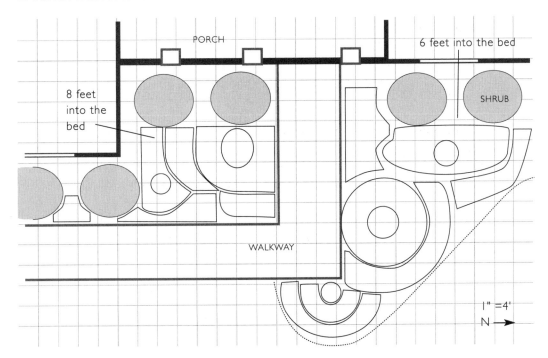

▲ How will anyone be able to reach and weed 6 or 8 feet into the bed shown here? Where will the caretaker stand while pruning the shrubs? Don't expect anyone to be able to reach more than 2 to 3 feet into a bed to weed.

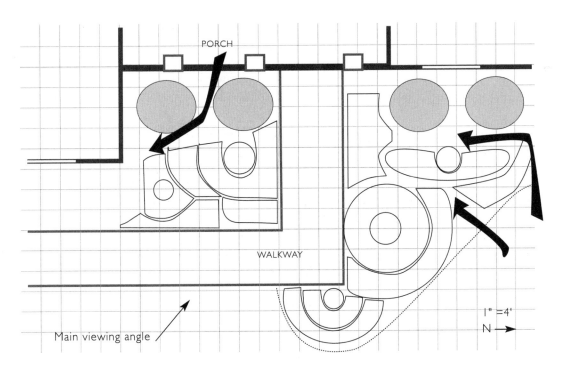

▲ Provide places to stand and ways to get to those places. Reduce the size or shift some frames to create paths for the caretaker. Place such paths across the main viewer's field of vision, rather than parallel to it.

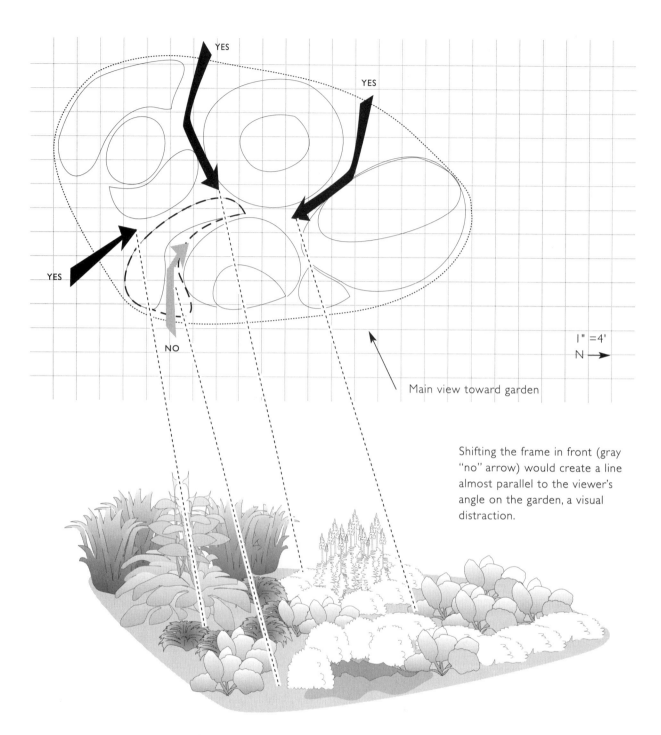

YES

YES

YES

NO

Main view toward garden

1" = 4'

N →

Shifting the frame in front (gray "no" arrow) would create a line almost parallel to the viewer's angle on the garden, a visual distraction.

▲ Make the most of those "bare" spaces in the bed. Here, the caretaker can easily get right into the center of the bed. All areas are accessible from a working path or the lawn, no more than 2 or 3 feet away. Openings already between plant groups are used for paths. The paths can be mulched, laid with stepping stones, or planted with a low ground cover that can take some foot traffic.

Don't make extra work for your caretaker. If an overhead sprinkler will be used in this garden, see if you can finagle a clear space to set it where most of the garden can be sprinkled in one arc. This clear area shouldn't be surrounded by tall plants that would block the low, wide-angle spray meant to wet the edges of the garden. I usually find a place where the hose can be dragged in along a working path and the sprinkler set in the bed itself, between groups of low- or medium-height plants.

THINK ABOUT MOWERS

Did you identify a potential mower or traffic problem back in the early stages of this design? Do something to protect your investment in this masterpiece, while it's still just a drawing board issue. Here's how to make a friend of the mowing crew, or at least avoid starting a war:

When there's foot traffic to think about, see whether you can tell where it will go in relation to this new garden. If the garden ended up straddling someone's path, see whether you can supply an adequate detour. Open up a space between focal point groups. Draw in stepping-stones. People, even little ones, are more accommodating than animals. If you foresee an animal traffic problem, specify fencing.

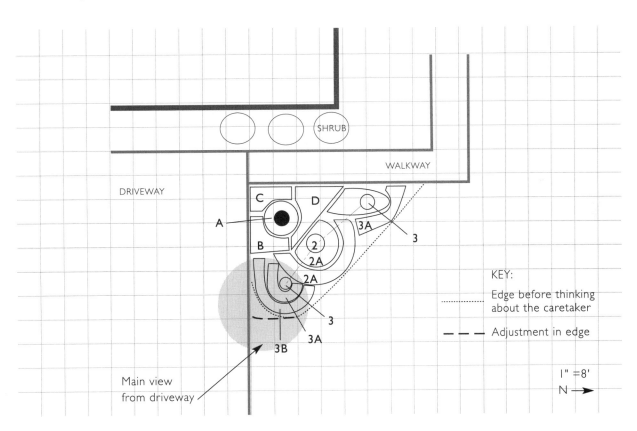

▲ Check for edges that cannot be negotiated when mowing. Find alternatives for strips of lawn narrower than the mower's wheel base, narrow peninsulas, and isolated islands of sod. Here, the line that leaves the narrow peninsula of sod is not essential to the overall design; it can be eliminated.

The Final Test

Now set that list of reasons for the garden alongside the plants and features that have been used. You've made all other adjustments and changes. The design is done but for this last check, the most important one: Does the garden fulfill the goals?

I do this final check with a chart. Use the key on your drawing and make a goal-check chart. Each item in the key will be a row of the chart. Column headings will be the reasons for the garden, and they'll vary for every garden. Let's take as an example a garden that is meant to have color and interest all year and attract birds and butterflies.

Lay a sheet of paper next to the key on your design. List the plants and important nonplant features in the garden in the key, as in the example below.

	butterflies	FLOWERS OR INTEREST:								
		Winter	Mar.	Apr.	May	June	July	Aug.	Sept.	Oct.
Zinnia	✓					✓	✓	✓	✓	
Lantana	✓					✓	✓	✓	✓	
Pincushion flower	✓					✓	✓	✓		
Lavender	✓	✓				✓				
Thyme		✓				✓				
Maiden grass		✓							✓	✓
'Palace Purple' coral bells		✓				✓				
Aster	✓							✓	✓	
Black-eyed Susan	✓						✓	✓		
Butterfly bush	✓							✓	✓	
Pearly everlasting							✓	✓	✓	
Birdbath	✓	✓	✓	✓	✓	✓	✓	✓	✓	✓

▲ Check your finished design against the goals. The flowers, plus the birdbath, come pretty close to meeting this garden's goals: flower color or interest all year, attracting birds and butterflies. As a result of this final check, though, the designer can see that spring color is lacking. Perhaps the spring-blooming plants were all dropped in adjustments along the way. It's simple to fill the gap with spring bulbs, or replace a June-blooming plant with a spring bloomer of similar height, shape, and texture.

You may have to add some features to your key at this point. Draw columns and label them for the months of the growing season, winter, birds, and butterflies. Then place a check or note in each column in which an item in the key meets a garden goal. A check in the winter column means the plant is interesting in winter; that is, it is evergreen, or sturdy, attractive seed pods remain during winter. A note in the butterfly column identifies the plant as a larval food for caterpillars or as a nectar source for adults. The birdbath is checked as an attraction for birds.

This system works well if the goals columns are appropriate. The designer knows the main reasons for the garden, and what has been done to this point to fulfill them. Only the goals that are still in doubt need to be checked. For instance, most of my gardens require continuous bloom and use a lot of perennials, so a column for each growing season month is almost standard for me. But in some cases, I decide in Step 5 to use primarily annuals, so there's no need to check for month-by-month bloom.

Look for gaps and weak areas on the chart. How could such a thing happen, after all your careful attention? It just does. In one case, I knew full well that the owners felt that yellow was the most worthless color in the world.

"Death to yellow!" they had said to me. So where did those two yellow flowers come from, in the end? Don't be hard on yourself for this kind of thing; just make whatever changes you can. Let's say the dried flower column of the chart is blank. Maybe there were plants on the plant list back in Step 5 that could have provided dried flowers, but they were all overlooked or lost to changes along the way. Now, a plant in the design must be identified as expendable and a dried flower plant found that will serve in its place, or a place must be found where a plant can be added.

To replace a plant, find a plant that matches all the characteristics of the plant that is being replaced, as well as those that fulfill the missing goal. If the reason for the replacement is to add color in a certain month, this may be a matter of selecting a later or earlier blooming variety of some species of plant already in the design. If the designer's purpose is to introduce winter interest or to add a cooking herb to the garden, the existing and replacement plants may be different species though they are similar in height, shape, and texture.

Look down. Is that a finished design on the table? Congratulations! Give yourself a good pat on the back and enjoy that garden!

Where to Go from Here

Congratulations! You have now completed your first official landscape design. Doesn't that feel good? Now that you've gotten your feet wet, so to speak, the best thing you can do is keep learning and planning. With each passing season, you'll become more accomplished and your designs will become better and better. In this section, I'll show you how to stay on that learning curve.

Get to Know More about Plants

There is no direct replacement for time when it comes to getting to know a plant. Whether you study the plant in a book or go out into a botanical garden to get acquainted with it, that method won't tell you all. That's because people have different opinions, plants act differently in different places, and plants are living things that change over a season.

Working only from books, it is difficult to learn enough about a plant to envision it in a design. Photographs can be misleading. An author's concept of "beauty" might be different from yours, and so a plant that rated a glowing report in a book seems ugly in your garden.

Seeing a plant even in the most fabulous garden around will not prepare you for how the plant will look in *your* garden. There have been times when I placed a plant that was new to me in what seemed like the identical conditions in which I had seen it growing, yet the plant did not grow nearly the same for me as at that other place.

Then there is the problem of what I call "Cinderella plants," beautiful one week, pale shadows of themselves the next. How can you know that new plant you just put into your main focal point won't fade miserably later in the season?

TAKE THE SMART APPROACH

Here's what you can do to minimize the surprises when you design with plants you haven't grown before.

Read about the plant in at least two sources. If you find disagreement between those sources, go to a third to break the tie. I'm not telling you the third author will be right, just telling you to hedge your bets.

Go see the plant growing. Botanical gardens are good for this, because these are teaching gardens as opposed to display gardens. Plants there have labels. In the library there are books that list public gardens throughout the United States, including their telephone numbers, hours of operation, and often a map to help you find your way. Call ahead and check whether plants in the garden are labeled or whether someone on the staff could help you when you get there. If you don't have such a place nearby, do you have a friend or neighbor who gardens who might be able to show you the plant? You might also put your plant identification book under your arm and go to a public display garden, such as in a zoo or city park. The problem with this last option is that the pictures in the book may not show you enough of the plant for you to make a positive identification.

Why not go to a nursery? Fine, if the nursery has a display garden. Don't try to learn about a plant from those that are potted for sale, though. You would be amazed at the manipulation that goes into keeping those plants saleable. Some are started early in the season, in a greenhouse, much earlier than you ever could manage in your garden. This is done so they will be in bloom for early spring sales. Others are kept clipped back or in cold storage to stall off their bloom. How can you know, then, whether you can depend on the plant to be blooming at this same time of year in your garden? Plants that have a tendency to be ugly may be pruned back to stubs and removed from the sales area until they become more presentable. Very rarely will you see a mature plant for sale, and just like puppies, all baby plants are endearing. So stick to bona fide gardens when you attempt to see what the plant looks and acts like.

Use all your senses. Touch the plant; smell its leaves and flowers. You may find something you like or dislike that was not mentioned in your book. Children have taught me more about plants than any book ever will, because they do not hesitate to use all their senses around the garden. When a bus full of kindergarteners descends on a garden, nothing escapes attention. The kids may be so full of questions that even the most experienced gardener will feel very humble.

Note sun and soil conditions. Decide whether the plant looks healthy, a simple thing to do if you can get your eyes off its flowers for a minute. Leaves tell about a plant's well-being just as skin does on people. Who among us has not said at one time or another, "Gee, you look pale," or "You sure are flushed!" Limp leaves that are not a uniform color are not usually happy leaves.

If you can find a gardener, ask questions. If necessary, volunteer to help rake or pull weeds while you talk. Most gardeners love to talk to other gardeners. The only time they might be unhelpful is when they are extremely busy (perhaps because some production-oriented, nongardening supervisor is leaning on them to increase their number of square feet weeded per hour). Ask whether the plant needs any special pruning or staking, whether it is plagued by particular diseases or pests, and how often the garden gets watered. There's a wealth of information there.

OFF-SEASON STUDIES

Many gardeners do their designing during the winter. Not a great time to go see the plant really growing, you say? Think again. World-class amusement parks and gardens in the southern and western United States are horticultural treasure chests. My children refuse to visit them any more without a signed contract from me, swearing that their father and I will not spend all our time inspecting gardens and tagging along after gardeners.

Is travel not within your means? Then turn to garden magazines, large-format garden books, and calendars with garden pictures. Leaf through a stack of these in your library after you've done your preliminary research on a plant. I'll bet you can find a picture of that plant in a magazine or book if you look long enough. It's a wonderful way to learn, because at a glance you see the plant and get clues to what grows well with it. Don't use such sources to judge growing conditions, though. The garden in the photo may look very sunny to you, but the photographer may have waited all day for enough light to snap the shutter.

TAKE YOUR BEST SHOT

When you feel you have a worthwhile plant, use it. Work with only those characteristics of the plant you are sure of: height or flower color, for instance. You may decide to replace or move a few plant species in your design after a year, but the majority of your choices will be keepers.

Planting from a Design

Once, when I was away with my husband, fellow gardeners laid out the beds we had just designed for a longtime customer. This customer has always enjoyed working with us in his gardens and arranged to take a week's vacation to be a part of this latest project. The new beds were extensive. It required our whole crew plus the owner to plot out the curves, remove sod, and double dig the beds. It was done with precision. Where the design called for a bend 6 feet long, jutting out 18 inches, so it was. The gardeners were rightfully pleased with all their work, none more than the owner himself, full of newly discovered talent with both tape measure and spade.

That design had materialized in my head. It had never before existed in the real world. When I arrived, with plants and my planting tools in tow, I saw that a few adjustments needed to be made; a few others could be made that would make the garden even better than I had dreamed. Did we make those adjustments or improvements? Not on your life. They stayed in my head. The investment that had already gone into those curves, that meticulously turned soil, those relocated sprinkler heads, more than outweighed the benefits my tinkering might bring. That garden is truly beautiful and loved. Yet each time I see it, I enjoy it in the shadow of what could have been.

SWAP YOUR PENCIL FOR YARD-MARKING TOOLS

When it's time to plant out your design, be there. Get a can of spray paint, some stakes and string, bonemeal, or even white flour that you can use to transfer the design from paper to the earth without breaking ground.

In a new yard, one with no lawn, you can even scratch out an outline with a stick. Go to a second-story window and direct a helper as he or she scratches a line in the soil, spray paints an edge, or places stakes and string. Or you can cut a hole in the corner of a bag of bonemeal and walk the edge of the bed, then check it from the main viewpoint. If you want the garden to live up to your vision, be sure to check how it looks — don't rely on the opinions of others.

Often I read about using a garden hose to lay out an edge and make adjustments before digging. This has never worked for me. In the spring, when we do most of our brand-new beds, hoses are too cold and stiff to make smooth curves. I find that rope works better, as long as it's not stiff nylon.

Doggone It!

Do you have a dog? Don't use bonemeal as a marker if you do. Dogs love to roll in bonemeal, snuffle it, dig where they smell it, even grab the bag out of your hands and dash around the yard, leaving white trails behind them. I'm not sure whether bonemeal is good for the dog, but the mess it leaves behind can be infuriating to the designer.

A FINAL COUNTDOWN

When the edge becomes reality and the soil is dug and settling, get a stack of empty pots. Spray paint a key letter on the bottom of each pot, so that when the pot is turned upside down, it proclaims "A" for aster or "D" for dahlia. Mark enough pots so you have one for every large perennial plant and six-pack of annuals in your first focal point group. If you have the actual plants on hand, leave them in their pots and use them instead of empty pots as placeholders. Set the pots or plants out according to your design and stand back at the main viewpoint. Walk around to the secondary viewpoints. Manipulate the placeholders as you see fit. When all is well, use the spray paint, bonemeal, or flour to outline each group of plants.

If you have help, don't let anyone stand idle. Let others use the scale drawing. They can measure to each plant's location and set up placeholders for your approval.

YOU'RE THE EXPERT

Don't be apologetic as you move placeholders around and hear or sense others' judgments. Exercise your artistic prerogatives with dignity and humor. Advise scoffers to read this book, if they want to begin to understand all the variables you're taking into account as you work. Don't be overly sensitive, either. Remember all the different viewpoints and interests you incorporated in this design. Consider whether your helpers' critiques might represent an opportunity: to learn, to educate, to improve. One time, a man voiced the opinion that all my maneuvering of rocks was a waste of time, as far as he could see, and couldn't we get to the planting and be done with it? I bit back my initial urge to suggest that perhaps he lug the large rocks around for me if he wanted it done more quickly. Instead, I fell back

on the design I believed in, and explained that the rocks would be all that would be of interest for half of each year, and I thought it was worth the effort. One day in January, I got a call from that man. He wanted to tell me that he really liked to look out the window at that garden.

Move to each focal point and use your placeholders to lay out plants and make adjustments. When you are confident of all the plant locations, plant!

Rearranging an Existing Garden

Many of us who love to garden become collectors of plants. Your garden may be chock-full of plants, most of them perennials and self-sowing annuals acquired over years. At some point you will probably feel the need to redesign that garden. Here's some advice.

RETURN TO STEP 1

Think through Step 1, your reason for the garden (see page 5). Obviously, you want a garden to experience variety. List any other reasons; you'll need them when you add or cull plants.

It's probably useless to retrace Steps 2 and 3 — you're already doing the maintenance and have already spent the money! There may be some worth in thinking about your time budget, though. You can redesign the whole bed on paper, no matter how large, in a few hours. Actually moving the plants takes longer. I don't try to redo more than 50 square feet of my own gardens in any one weekend.

BOW TO FATHER TIME

Assess the site (see Step 4 on page 21). No kidding. Especially if you have been gardening this site for quite some time, take a look at what it has become. Time passes quickly for gardeners. That's why when a longtime gardener assures me that his or her private garden is in the full sun, I'm not surprised when I see it and realize it is in half sun or even a shady spot. Gardeners may be so in tune with their botanical cohabitants that they can no more see aging there than in life-long human friends. A sapling tree contributes just a little more shade each year. After 10 or 15 years, though still a baby in the eyes of its gardener, it's top dog in its site. Soil can also become worn out, degenerating almost imperceptibly each year from a nice sandy loam to a silty loam in need of organic matter. New privacy fences, walkways, and building projects of all sorts may have created problems, such as blocking water and impeding air movement.

INVENTORY PLANTS

Make a list of all the plants you have. Group them by shapes and textures. I find it easiest to do this as an inventory, in chart format, while I'm standing out in the garden.

Although you should, I won't ask you to eliminate any plants. I know you won't. I will warn you that you're probably going to end up with orphans, divisions from thinning existing plants, and whole plants whose species didn't fit into the new plan. You will end up creating a whole new garden for these misfits, overly prolific species, and ne'er-do-wells. Either that or your surplus plant gifts will be the beginning of a neighbor's or family member's plant collection!

Pay absolutely no attention to the quantities or present locations of your plants. List only plant names, shapes, textures, and uses on your list, just as in Step 5 (see page 53).

DON'T FIGHT IT — SCALE IT

Measure the existing garden. Decide whether you will treat it as one garden or several different gardens. The key to this decision may be (oh no, not again!) the main viewer location. Draw the garden(s) to scale.

FOLLOW THE DESIGN

Pick a main focal point for the garden, or one in each sub-garden (see Step 6 on page 71). Select one favorite plant to be a focal point plant or the first frame around the nonplant focal point, as appropriate.

Go inside, sit down where you cannot see the garden, and compose several focal point groups from your inventory list. When it becomes difficult to compose the next group, it may be time to add a new plant to your plant list. Most likely, you will find it necessary to search for plants of a certain shape or texture previously underrepresented in your garden.

Stay inside as you design. This is a time to be heartless, using only plants whose shape, texture, or use commend them. If you go outside, plants of low value in this new design will play on your sympathies and wheedle themselves an undeserved space in the new order. Work through all the steps for framing the focal point and selecting secondary focal point locations. Use the groups you concocted at each secondary focal point.

KEEP AN OPEN MIND

When it comes to outlining the garden, keep an open mind. Should the bed be changed? Could it be? Think of me, and my once-in-a-lifetime turn at the lawn mower. This might be your chance to get input from all the significant others, maybe even gain a gardening buddy.

Don't overlook making adjustments, especially for the caretaker. Sure, you've been using an old shovel handle as an extension for your hand-hoe for years, but that doesn't mean you have to keep doing that. Build in working space. I'll bet you have a lot of plants that can handle some foot traffic!

WORK IN MANAGEABLE CHUNKS

Now take a deep breath. Get a drink of water. Put on your gloves. Go dig up everything within the entire first focal point area, or 100 square feet of that focal point area, whichever comes first.

Take a healthy rootball with each plant. If some of these plants didn't make the cut and won't be in the redesigned bed, move them immediately to their new homes. If some of the plants will be used in the new bed but not in this focal point group, put them in a side bed where they will be safe for a few weeks. (Come on, we collectors all have nooks and crannies where we temporarily stash plants.) Put the keeper plants in pots or in plastic garbage bags in the shade, mist them daily, and don't worry about them. I often keep plants on hold in this fashion for as much as two weeks, even plant species that "resent transplanting," even at the height of midsummer. Those plants have been around long enough to know that you're not trying to kill them. They'll wait while you renew the soil.

As you put the plants back into their new places, space them widely rather than crowding. Move in plants from other parts of the garden, as called for in your design.

Take a rest for a few days or a week. Redoing an existing garden is exhausting work, much more tiring than making a new garden. Getting a new bed ready, the gardener throws thousands of grass plants around without a thought, mercilessly killing every root encountered. In redoing a garden, every plant or root you touch cries out to you: "Can I stay, please?" "Wait! Are you sure you know what you're doing!" "Don't mistake me for a weed root, I'm a precious gem of a plant!" No wonder you're drained.

When you've recovered from the first spate of planting, do a second focal point area. Then another, and another. This may sound crazy, but I know you'll have fun the whole while.

Branching Out: Design Whole Landscapes

As I mentioned at the beginning of this book, the same design steps that help you make beautiful gardens also apply to landscape design. Below I guide you in the three areas — budget, scale, and edges — in which you may need help to make a smooth transition from flowering, knee-high garden cuties to 80-foot focal points and 8-foot landscape fillers.

BUDGET

Landscapes don't cost as much as you may think. As a matter of fact, they cost the same or less per square foot as a perennial garden. Be sure to set yourself a dollar budget and break your design up into doable sections so you feel good about completing each phase.

There's a saying, "Every long journey begins with a single step." Be realistic about what you can accomplish in a given length of time. Design and finish one area. Then step back, admire it, and watch it for a season or two. It can tell you where to go next. That is, it will tell you whether you can wait!

Patience helps. I remember explaining a design concept to Curt, one of my dearest friends and best customers, early in our relationship. In my hand was the drawing that would remake a huge, existing flower bed. The house is on a corner lot and we were standing in the middle of the intersection of two side streets, looking toward the garden and the front of the house. The bed is out away from the house, in a deep easement, bound by two straight public sidewalks, a driveway, and the road. It completely fills the easement, 20 feet wide and 70 or 80 feet deep. On the house side of the sidewalk was only lawn plus a couple of foundation shrubs.

I was explaining to Curt how I wanted this disconnected, beautiful garden to become more a part of his yard. Curt's a humble person and loves to garden for its own sake. He doesn't necessarily care whether he gets credit for his horticultural accomplishments. It was my idea to be sure everyone would know for certain that this garden was not some off-track city project but the work of a private individual. From the focal point, which is a wondrous fossilized coral boulder planted with dozens of rock plants, I had used frames and plant groups to draw a line that pointed toward Curt's front porch. It was not a straight line but a slow, deliberate curve like the arm of a pinwheel. Even though the garden itself stopped abruptly at the public sidewalk, the viewer on the street would finish a visual tour of the garden with the understanding that the owner of that home to the left was responsible for it all. For Curt, sitting on his stool on the front porch, his end of the line would lead back to his beloved rock.

The landscape evolved. This line was, of course, not in existence at the time of our conversation. I waved my arms around and tried to describe how things would look. Curt nodded and approved the plan. Months later, the redesign work done, I was on to other projects when Curt called. Could I come

over and look at another area for him? What he showed me were two areas, one between the sidewalk and the house, and one on the far side of the front yard from the redesigned garden. He had gotten to looking at that pinwheel line, liked it, and wanted to define its path more clearly right up to his porch plus make the logical extension out along a second arm, to a new bed in the far front yard. His yard is beautiful, and it has evolved a piece at a time in just this way.

It's a fact of life that not everyone has Curt's deliberate patience, though. Marjory, another great friend and customer, asked me for a plan for her new yard. We talked about what she wanted and built the design on the understanding that it would be completed in stages over several years. Since this was the third house I had gardened with Marjory, I should have known to accelerate the timetable for planting. Marjory decided that the expense was not such a burden as the wait, and before I was really ready, we were done with that plan and were on to additional beds.

If you're somewhere in between the Curts and Marjorys in temporal demands, you will need to prioritize your landscaping efforts. Here's the best piece of advice I have for you: Don't start with places in the yard that bother you, start with places that will give you pleasure when you look at them.

SCALE

You probably have a scale survey of your property that came with the purchase, so working up scale drawings will be easy to do. The scale I refer to now is one of increased plant dimension and field of vision.

Trees and shrubs have distinct shapes and textures, just as annual and perennial flowers do. They also have distinct, large mature sizes and a tendency to grow much more quickly than expected, once they've settled in.

When you set them down on your eagle-eye drawing and try them out here and there, be sure you know just how much room they actually need. If you select a tree for its beautiful round crown, so distinctive when flush with blossoms, be sure to give that plant room to develop fully. Crowding means losing quality in individual plant shape.

There are many good plant encyclopedias that list trees and shrubs as well as annuals and perennials. Use one that tells you the mature spread of the plant. If you won't be in your home for the 15 or 20 years it may take for the plant to reach maturity, and don't care how the plants look after you're gone, use a book that gives you the growth rate for the species, and pick one that will not outgrow its space during your tenure.

Think big. Don't confine yourself to 25- and 30-foot widths in the areas you design. A single average crabapple spreads 20 feet. Its first frame of plants may best be displayed in an arc 8 or 10 feet out from its trunk. The secondary focal points that frame the crabapple group may be 40 and 50 feet away in opposite directions.

Work first with the largest plants in your landscape. Place the trees and shrub groups. Use ground covers, perennials, and annuals only as the outer frames and fillers for these groups. Designate a few high-visibility areas just for gardens, and design those separately. Certainly those gardens can pick up themes and highlights from the rest of the landscape, but it's not essential that they do. It may be in keeping with your reasons for landscaping to repeat a tree-shrub focal point group in a nearby flower bed, in miniature — for example, a round crabapple accompanied by mounded bird's-nest spruces and coarse yuccas, reducing to cushion spurge surrounded by Stokes aster, and flanked by miniature daylilies. If it doesn't serve one of your landscape purposes to relate everything in this way, don't. Just place plants, frame, more plants, more frame, and have a good time doing it.

EDGES AND ENDS

Work extra hard at waiting until Step 11 (see page 121) to outline beds in the landscape. It makes me sad to see pretty trees and shrubs crowded within an area just because the beds were outlined before the plants were selected and placed. Don't use the dimensions of a neighbor's beds as a guideline. Your landscape will be different, better than the neighbor's, because it was designed specifically for you.

We have a tough time breaking away from the hard lines architects and builders give us. Concentrate on ignoring the prefab beds, corners, and bays when you first begin your design. Jump out across walkways and extend beds into the lawn. Ignore the corner of the house, if it's not worth framing. Don't feel compelled to design something for that 18-inch-wide strip along the porch under the eaves. Remember that anything between the viewer and the horizon can screen the horizon. You'll be amazed at how well groups of shrubs out in the yard or in deep beds around the house can hide a foundation even though they don't line up precisely 3 feet in front of the offending concrete.

Finally, I think you'll be astounded at how much you can accomplish and how quickly the designing will be done. Good luck!

Tools for Learning More

Recommended Reading

Probably the only things I value as much as plants are plant books. Here are some that I use when I search for the plants that go into my designs. Some are specialty encyclopedias; I think you'll be able to tell these from the general-purpose books by the titles.

Because I recommend these books doesn't mean they are the only ones that could be of use to you, or even that they are the best. View the books on this list just as you would view the items found in a well-loved toolbox: worn from use, maybe a little soiled from the most recent use, not new but not worn out, maybe not the best available of their kind but certainly serviceable. There are dozens more that might be on this list if I could afford them. If a good book that you come across is not on this list, use it. Maybe you'd like to send me a copy, too!

Armitage, Allan M. *Herbaceous Perennial Plants.* Athens, GA: Varsity Press, Inc., 1989.

———. *Butterfly Gardening.* San Francisco: Xerces Society in Association with the Smithsonian Institution, 1990.

———. "How to Landscape for Birds." *Gardening for Wildlife.* Brooklyn: Brooklyn Botanic Garden, Inc., 1987.

———. "A Garden Fit for Hummingbirds." *Gardening for Wildlife.* Brooklyn: Brooklyn Botanic Garden, Inc., 1987.

———. "Host Plant Index." *Audubon Society Field Guide to North American Butterflies.* New York: Chanticleer Press, Inc., 1981.

Art, Henry W. *A Garden of Wildflowers.* Pownal, VT: Storey Books, 1986.

Binetti, Marianne. *Tips for Carefree Landscapes.* Pownal, VT: Storey Books, 1990.

Brickell, Christopher, Editor-in-Chief. *The American Horticulture Society Encyclopedia of Garden Plants.* New York: MacMillan, 1990

Clausen, Ruth Rogers, and Nicolas H. Ekstrom. *Perennials for American Gardens.* New York: Random House, Inc., 1989.

Cox, Jeff, and Marilyn Cox. *The Perennial Garden.* Emmaus, PA: Rodale Press, Inc., 1985.

*Dirr, Michael A. *Manual of Woody Landscape Plants.* Champaign, IL: Stipes Publishing Company, 1990.

Fell, Derek. *The Essential Gardener.* New York: Michael Freedman Publishing Group, Inc., 1990.

Ferguson, Nicola. *Right Plant, Right Place.* New York: Summit Books, 1984.

Foerster, Karl. *Rock Gardens through the Year.* New York: Sterling Publishing Co., Inc., 1987.

Glattstein, Judy. *Garden Design with Foliage.* Pownal, VT: Storey Books, 1991.

Harper, Pamela. *Perennials, How to Select, Grow, and Enjoy.* Tucson, AZ: HPBooks, 1985.

Heriteau, Jacqueline. *The American Horticultural Society Flower Finder.* New York: Simon & Schuster, 1992.

————. *National Arboretum Book of Outstanding Garden Plants.* New York: Stonesong Press, 1990.

Hill, Lewis, and Nancy Hill. *Daylilies.* Pownal, VT: Storey Books, 1991.

————. *Successful Perennial Gardening.* Pownal, VT: Storey Books, 1988.

Macqueen, Sheila. *Flower Arranging from Your Garden.* Radnor, PA: Chilton Books, 1977.

Macunovich, Janet. *Caring for Perennials: What to Do and When to Do It.* Pownal, VT: Storey Books, 1996.

Paterson, Allen. *Plants for Shade and Woodland.* Markham, ON: Fitzhenry & Whiteside, Ltd., 1987.

Phillips, Roger, and Martyn Rix. *The Random House Book of Perennials, Volume I, Early Perennials.* New York: Random House, 1991.

————. *The Random House Book of Perennials, Volume II, Late Perennials.* New York: Random House, 1991.

————. *The Random House Book of Roses.* New York: Random House, 1988.

————. *The Random House Book of Shrubs.* New York: Random House, 1989.

Reinhardt, Thomas A., Martina Reinhardt, and Mark Moskowitz. *Ornamental Grass Gardening.* Los Angeles: HPBooks, 1989.

Rice, Graham. *Plants for Problem Places.* Portland, OR: Timber Press, Inc., 1988.

Runkel, Sylvan T., and Dean M. Roosa. *Wildflowers of the Tallgrass Prairie: The Upper Midwest.* Ames, IA: Iowa State University Press, 1989.

Schenk, George. *The Complete Shade Gardener.* Boston: Houghton Mifflin Co., 1984.

————. *Color with Annuals.* San Francisco: Ortho Books, 1987.

Silber, Mary, and Terry Silber. *The Complete Book of Everlastings.* New York: Alfred A. Knopf, 1987.

Sinnes, A. Cort. *All About Perennials.* San Francisco: Ortho Books, 1981.

Still, Steven. *Manual of Herbaceous Ornamental Plants.* Champaign, IL: Stipes Publishing Company, 1988.

Taylor's Guide to Annuals. New York: Houghton Mifflin, Inc., 1986.

Taylor's Guide to Bulbs. New York: Houghton Mifflin, Inc., 1986.

Taylor's Guide to Ground Covers, Vines, and Grasses. New York: Houghton Mifflin, Inc., 1986.

Taylor's Guide to Perennials. New York: Houghton Mifflin, Inc., 1986.

Thomas, Graham Stuart. *Plants for Ground-Cover.* Portland, OR: Sagapress, Inc./Timber Press, Inc., 1990.

Wright, Michael. *The Complete Book of Gardening.* New York: Warner Books, 1979.

*This book does not contain traditional annual and perennial flowers, but it is valuable for information about vines, some ground cover plants, and, especially, trees and shrubs.

CATALOGS

There are many lovely and useful mail-order supplier catalogs. For a complete list of companies, write to the Mailorder Gardening Association or visit their web site at www.mailordergardening.com or write to P.O. Box 2129, Columbia, MD 21045.

USDA Hardiness Zone Map

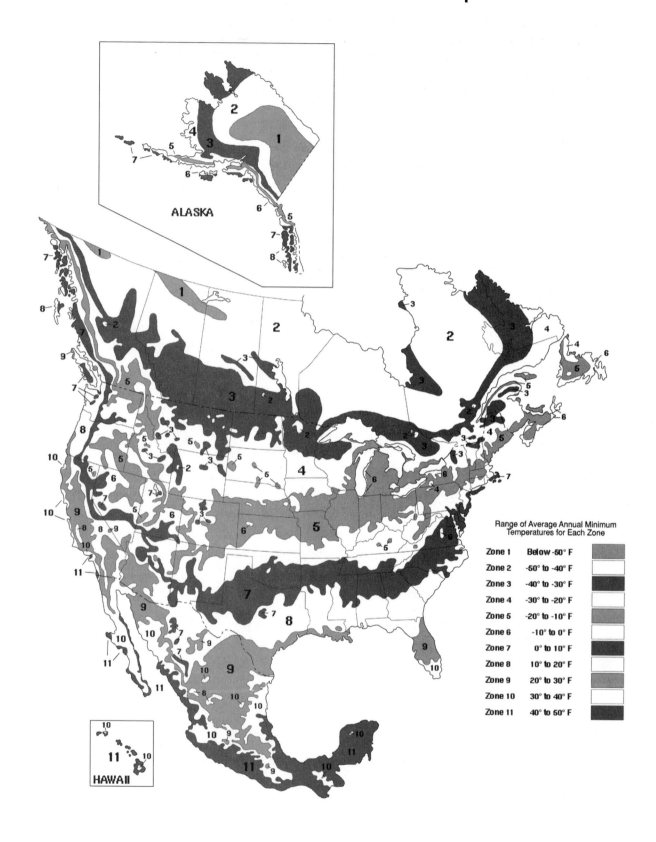

Range of Average Annual Minimum
Temperatures for Each Zone

Zone	Temperature
Zone 1	Below -50° F
Zone 2	-50° to -40° F
Zone 3	-40° to -30° F
Zone 4	-30° to -20° F
Zone 5	-20° to -10° F
Zone 6	-10° to 0° F
Zone 7	0° to 10° F
Zone 8	10° to 20° F
Zone 9	20° to 30° F
Zone 10	30° to 40° F
Zone 11	40° to 50° F

USDA Plant Hardiness Zone Map

The United States Department of Agriculture (USDA) created the map opposite to give gardeners a helpful tool for selecting and cultivating plants. The map divides North America into 11 zones, based on each area's average minimum temperature. Areas in Zone 1 are the coldest and in Zone 11, the warmest. Determine your zone, and then use that information to select plants that are most likely to thrive in your climate.

Metric Conversion Chart

When the measurement given is	To convert it to	Multiply it by
miles	kilometers	1.6
inches	centimeters	2.54
feet	meters	0.305
gallons	liters	3.785
pounds	kilograms	0.45

Planning Tools

Use the planning sheets on the following pages to help you create your dream landscape. You have the publisher's permission to make copies of the sheets before filling them in so you'll have a ready supply. Just add a pencil, eraser, and tape measure, and you're ready to plan.

SITE ASSESSMENT SHEET

The view
■ area is seen mainly from:_____

dominating existing features	color	shape	texture	effect

■ background could be:_____
■ strong lines are:_____
■ overall feeling is:_____
■ good location for a garden:_____

Sunlight
■ hours per day of direct sun: sun (6 hrs or more)   half sun (4–6 hrs)   shade (2–4 hrs)   dense shade (0-2 hrs)
■ sunny hours: 8   9   10   11   NOON   1   2   3   4   5   6   7
■ seasonal differences in sun at this spot:_____

Soil
■ texture: sandy   sandy loam   loam   clay loam   clay   silty loam   silt
■ aeration: loose   firm   compacted
■ health of existing plants: good   poor   Notes:_____
■ depth of existing roots: deep   shallow   Notes:_____

Water availability
■ natural water
   ■ blockers:_____
   ■ depth of water table:_____
■ irrigation via
   ■ automatic system: spray jets   misters   soakers/bubblers   Notes:_____
   ■ manual system: notes:_____
■ drainage: very fast   average   poor   standing water   Notes:_____
■ runoff from:_____

Root competition
■ garden would share root space with:_____
■ existing plants that would have to be excluded:_____

Exposure
■ natural: wind   extreme heat   frost
■ man-made
   recreational activities:_____   foot traffic:_____
   pets:_____   other:_____

Index

Note: **Boldface** numbers indicate charts; *italic* numbers indicate illustrations.

Other Storey Titles You Will Enjoy

Caring for Perennials, by Janet Macunovich. A month-by-month approach to perennial gardening. Includes care charts for more than 130 perennials. 200 pages. Paperback. ISBN 1-88266-957-5.

Landscaping Makes Cents, by Frederick C. Campbell and Richard L. Dubé. A complete guide to adding substantial value and beauty to a home through careful landscape design. 176 pages. Paperback. ISBN 0-88266-948-6.

The Lawn & Garden Owner's Manual, by Lewis and Nancy Hill. What to do and when to do it. How to diagnose and cure lawn and garden problems, rejuvenate neglected landscaping, and maintain beautiful and healthy grounds. 192 pages. Paperback. ISBN 1-58017-214-8.

Mulch It! A practical guide to using mulch in the garden and landscape, by Stu Campbell. Advice on every kind of mulch and on how to use mulches on everything from landscape plantings to vegetable gardens. 128 pages. Paperback. ISBN 1-58017-316-0.

Pruning Made Easy, by Lewis Hill. A gardener's visual guide to when and how to prune everything, from flowers to trees. 224 pages. Paperback. ISBN 1-58017-006-4.

Stonescaping, by Jan Kowalczewski Whitner. How to incorporate stone into many garden features including paths, steps, walls, ponds, and rock gardens. 20 basic designs. 168 pages. Paperback. ISBN 0-88266-755-6.

Storey's Basic Country Skills: A Practical Guide to Self-Reliance, by John and Martha Storey. More than 150 of Storey's expert authors in gardening, building, animal raising, and homesteading share their specialized knowledge and experience in this ultimate guide to living a more independent, satisfying life. Step-by-step, illustrated instructions for every aspect of country living. 544 pages. Paperback. ISBN 1-58017-199-0.

Successful Perennial Gardening, by Lewis and Nancy Hill. A user-friendly guide to the challenges and joys of perennial gardening. 240 pages. Paperback. ISBN 1-88266-472-7.

The Vegetable Gardener's Bible, by Edward C. Smith. Integrates four gardening techniques — wide rows, organic methods, raised beds, and deep soil — to grow high-yielding, healthy vegetable gardens. Contains all you need to know about pest and disease control, soil, compost, and how to grow more than 70 vegetables and herbs. 320 pages. 450 full-color photographs. Paperback. ISBN 1-58017-212-1.

Watering Systems for Lawn and Garden, by R. Dodge Woodson. A complete handbook for anyone wanting to buy or install a small-scale irrigation system for the lawn, garden, or backyard. 144 pages. Paperback. ISBN 0-88266-906-0.

*These and other Storey titles are available at your bookstore,
farm store, garden center, or directly from
Storey Books, 210 MASS MoCA Way, North Adams, MA 01247,
or by calling 1-800-441-5700. Visit our website at www.storey.com.*